BUILDING A BETTER BUSINESS USING THE LEGO® SERIOUS PLAY® METHOD

Per Kristiansen
Robert Rasmussen

WILEY

Cover illustration and design: C. Wallace

Published by John Wiley & Sons, Inc., Hoboken, New Jersey.
Published simultaneously in Canada.

For general information about our other products and services, please contact our Customer Care Department within the United States at (800) 762–2974, outside the United States at (317) 572–3993 or fax (317) 572–4002.

Wiley publishes in a variety of print and electronic formats and by print-on-demand. Some material included with standard print versions of this book may not be included in e-books or in print-on-demand. If this book refers to media such as a CD or DVD that is not included in the version you purchased, you may download this material at http://booksupport.wiley.com. For more information about Wiley products, visit www.wiley.com.

ISBN 978-1-118-83245-5 (pbk); ISBN 978-1-118-93136-3 (ebk); ISBN 978-1-118-93137-0 (ebk)

Printed in the United States of America
10 9 8 7 6 5 4 3 2

Contents

PART III LEGO® SERIOUS PLAY® at Work

Preface

Our aim in writing this book is to give you a hands-on introduction to the LEGO®
SERIOUS PLAY® method. We will explain why and how it was developed and what
theories came together in order to support it, and offer a number of examples of how
this approach has helped organizations all over the world. This book is not meant to be
a handbook that provides you with five easy steps to improve your business by using
the process. Rather, it is a journey into the world of LEGO SERIOUS PLAY.

With that in mind, you might be wondering: why read this book?

Well, you may read it because you have this nagging feeling that you are not
making the most of the potential with which you were born. Maybe you've observed
children—yours or other people's—at play, and wondered if there was a way to bring
the power of that interaction into organizations. Perhaps you believe that creativity is
a team process and you want to find a way to unlock it. Maybe you've simply observed
well-meaning individuals pulled in different directions in professional projects time
and again. Or perhaps you are simply curious about what this serious play thing is all
about.

Any of these are good reasons to read this book. We've made it our goal to help
you find answers to these issues—and, we hope, also to others that might emerge as
you read on.

But why did we decide to write this book now?

As you will find out in the Introduction, LEGO SERIOUS PLAY has traveled a
challenging path—one that has been far from straightforward. The business model
and supporting organization have changed numerous times. But perhaps the most
important challenge has been developing an understanding of what defines the
method. Eventually, the definition proved itself robust; and from this, it has become
clearer exactly what LEGO SERIOUS PLAY is, what it does, and how it can create
value for groups of people.

Naturally, this understanding will continue to evolve; more will become clear, and new learning will emerge. However, we have reached a sort of plateau at this point. It has been more than 10 years since we trained the first facilitators, and the method has been put to work in organizations of all sorts all over the world. It has been used by local governments, global service companies, big banks, start-ups, international manufacturing companies, and other entities. We will, throughout the book and in particular in Chapter 11, offer a varied set of examples. In short, LEGO SERIOUS PLAY is ready to share its story with a larger audience.

The next obvious question: why are *we* writing the story of LEGO SERIOUS PLAY?

Both together and on our own, we have been part of the story since its beginning. We have spent the past decade working on projects and initiatives intricately interwoven with LEGO SERIOUS PLAY.

We were part of developing the method when it was still a research idea, and managed it when it was owned by an independent company, Executive Discovery, and when it was a business unit inside LEGO. We developed and delivered the first facilitator training programs and the first facilitator manuals. Over the years, we've facilitated workshops and conducted training programs for teams all over the world, initially as employees of Executive Discovery and then of LEGO itself. We are now partners, and each owns and runs an organization that specializes in LEGO SERIOUS PLAY. Robert is the principal of Rasmussen Consulting and Per is a partner in Trivium, both headquartered in Denmark, and working globally with the method.

Our work remains focused on LEGO SERIOUS PLAY. We develop and deliver customized workshops to global organizations, and run facilitator certification programs in the method. These programs are also delivered globally and partly under the shared brand of "the Association of Master Trainers in the LEGO SERIOUS PLAY method." Finally, we act in an advisory function to LEGO, a role that allows us to work closely with the company to support the method's continued growth.

It is clear upon looking back at the history of LEGO SERIOUS PLAY that there have been moments when something special was required—when the approach needed practitioners, believers, friends, allies, ambassadors, and the tenacity of these people to survive and maintain momentum. Though there are countless examples, we will limit ourselves here to mentioning Kjeld Kirk Kristiansen, LEGO owner and the grandson of its founder. It was Kjeld Kirk Kristiansen's vision of a different way of leading that gave birth to LEGO SERIOUS PLAY. He has always seen the LEGO bricks as a language that can help unlock human potential, and he quickly realized that LEGO SERIOUS PLAY could bring that language into the boardroom. Kjeld Kirk Kristiansen's belief in the immense potential of the method has helped steady the ship several times. Without him, there would be no story to tell about LEGO SERIOUS PLAY, and, hence, this book would not have been possible.

Introduction—The Journey!

The LEGO® SERIOUS PLAY® method as we know it today is the result of a journey that took its first steps more than 15 years ago. It did not come about because of a conscious, long-term, premeditated strategy to expand the LEGO Company's reach into a new market segment. It was not the brainchild of a marketing department reacting to market demand or coming up with a new bright idea.

We call it LEGO SERIOUS PLAY today; but when it started, it didn't even have a name. It was as an idea for internal use, a wish for more imaginative ways of developing the company's strategic direction and plans, for unlocking the human potential in the organization.

Back in 1994, LEGO was—as it still is—a privately owned company. Owner Kjeld Kirk Kristiansen, whom we introduced in the Preface, was also the CEO of the company at the time. LEGO had being riding a wave of success for more than 20 years; the outlook for the future was bright. There were only a few dark clouds in the horizon. New toys like video games were entering the market, and children were playing differently; *growing older younger* was the term often used.

LEGO was starting to feel the impact of these changes, so Kirk Kristiansen naturally turned his attention to the ways and techniques that he and his leadership team used when developing their strategies. He was not very happy with the outcome of their sessions. While their business was about creativity and imagination, the way that they went about developing a new strategy and a new strategic direction felt decidedly *un*imaginative.

At the same time, professors Bart Victor and Johan Roos at IMD business school in Lausanne, Switzerland, were looking into different ways of creating strategies. LEGO had a close relationship with IMD for several years, as the business school played a significant role in the company's leadership development. Faculty members from IMD also provided consultancy for companies. Professors Victor and

Roos had experiences similar to Kirk Kristiansen's when it came to the quality of the traditional strategy development approaches for teams. Kristiansen connected with the two professors in 1996, and the three noted their similar frustration with traditional techniques for developing strategies. All three believed that:

- People are the key to an organization's success—and people *can* and *want to* do well.
- Strategy is something *you live*, not something stored away in a document.

Unfortunately, these tenets weren't playing; everyone did not live up to their full potential and the strategy was not something that could be lived. Kirk Kristiansen agreed to fund research on this conundrum by creating a separate LEGO subsidiary called Executive Discovery Ltd. The research would lead to a process where LEGO could use the approach internally, and the professors could advance their academic work in a real-world setting. Johan and Bart both had strong academic backgrounds in strategy making, complex adaptive systems, leadership, and organizational behavior. Executive Discovery Ltd. was created as the organization driving the research.

Over the next couple of years, the business school professors practiced their strategy concept using LEGO bricks instead of the usual methods of words, Post-it Notes, and whiteboards. The basic assumption was that if you threw a huge pile of bricks on the board table and asked people to "build their strategic ideas," their imaginations would flourish like children's—and the exercise would give life to the strategy-building concepts such as identity, landscape, and Simple Guiding Principles. These concepts remain an essential part of many LEGO SERIOUS PLAY applications to this day.

There was a lot of laughter and playing in the boardrooms during the first 45 minutes of these experimental sessions. However, something wasn't clicking. The bricks alone certainly did not result in new thinking and more imagination.

These discouraging experiences led to the first of many critical junctions for the LEGO SERIOUS PLAY method. Was this simply a bad idea that would never work—or was the formula missing something? There were some interesting strategy concepts, but no process for how to work with these using the bricks. In 1999, LEGO SERIOUS PLAY faced its first existential crisis.

But Executive Discovery's board decided not to give up quite yet. Instead, they asked Robert—who was director of research and development for LEGO Education at the time—if he would take a look at the feasibility of the LEGO SERIOUS PLAY idea. He agreed to do so while still continuing his job for LEGO Education. Later, his colleagues in Executive Discovery often remarked that he spent his time 100/100—100 percent on LEGO Education and 100 percent on LEGO SERIOUS PLAY.

Robert began investigating how he could apply his knowledge on how children learn and develop to an adult setting and strategy development. He and a small team of part-time freelancers set out to crack this code, and over a period of less than two years they developed the LEGO SERIOUS PLAY method. As they continued to work and build, the strategy concepts became more than just a theory. By 2001, the first version of LEGO SERIOUS PLAY was ready as "a thinking, communication, and problem solving technique for groups."

Reaching this goal took more than 20 iterations, tons of LEGO bricks, and the willingness of Robert's wife, Jette, to spend endless hours putting all of these bricks in small freezer bags for the trial kits. The IMD professors ran real-life sessions with companies using the prototypes. This helped confirm a pattern of working with the bricks that produced consistent results across different groups—the origin of the LEGO SERIOUS PLAY etiquette. By the end of 2001, the process was working consistently across different groups in a robust and reproducible way. It was also in 2001 that the first facilitators were trained and that a team was formed in order to support the method.

One of the themes that emerged from the development work was the value of getting groups to see the entire system that they were part of. This helped them envision scenarios and be better prepared for the future. By having a complete picture of their current system—a perspective that involved team roles, relationships, and culture—and testing the system with specific scenarios, team members gained more confidence, insight, and commitment in dealing with future events.

Very few people at LEGO even knew about the venture that Kjeld Kirk Kristiansen had embarked upon during the early days of SERIOUS PLAY. Nor did the development of the methodology happen within the physical walls of the LEGO Company in Denmark. Robert's base—LEGO Education's research and development—was located in a remote farmhouse in the state of Connecticut, United States. The second base was the Imagination Lab in Lausanne, Switzerland, from where Johan Roos, Bart Victor, and their team contributed with their theoretical knowledge and piloted the process and documentation.

More than 12 years have passed since the method was ready to go to market in late 2001. It has faced several existential challenges over the course of that decade, none of which were related to the quality of the process itself. Indeed, the approach has proven to be even more robust and generic than originally imagined.

A solid training model was in place by 2002, and we started to deliver programs for facilitators in the United States and Europe. In 2004, Per revised the LEGO SERIOUS PLAY training program for facilitators to emphasize further the fact that the method has a number of applications. In 2006 Robert defined and structured the Application Techniques with the purpose of making the process easier to apply to a broader range to topics within business, team, and personal development. Finally, in 2010, we restructured and enhanced the training program; with minor updates, this is the certification program that is being used today.

The struggles for LEGO SERIOUS PLAY from 2002 until 2010 involved questions on how to fit the business model into LEGO's value chain. Because the idea was Kjeld Kirk Kristiansen's brainchild and therefore very consistent with his values, by 2002 Executive Discovery Ltd. had changed from being the vehicle behind the research to owning both the methodology and the responsibility for bringing it to market.

In 2001, Executive Discovery Ltd., which had been a UK-registered company, closed, and Executive Discovery LLC (a U.S.-registered company) was established in Connecticut. Robert quit his job with LEGO Education and became COO for Executive Discovery LLC. Johan Roos and Bart Victor remained involved, respectively, in a board position and as part-time CEO, while they continued their academic careers.

Why this construction with Executive Discovery—a sister company to the LEGO Company—when the reality was that Kjeld Kirk Kristiansen provided all the funding and it was a LEGO product?

Kirk Kristiansen had four reasons for this approach. First, he knew that a small pet project like this would never fit into the company's streamlined mass production of toys. The marketing and manufacturing departments would immediately reject it. Second, it was very difficult to estimate the business potential. By keeping it small and outside mainstream LEGO, Kirk Kristiansen was able to minimize the risks. Third, he wanted this to be a long-lasting idea—not the "next big thing" or a fad taken up with great enthusiasm for only a brief period of time.

The fourth reason was the name "Executive Discovery." Kirk Kristiansen worried that the LEGO name could become a disadvantage rather than a leverage point, which might happen if the "toy" image turned people off instead of piquing their interest. Likewise, he wanted the initiative's name to signal that this was for the boardroom and corner office—the places where strategies were decided. The emphasis was on SERIOUS PLAY instead of *LEGO* SERIOUS PLAY.

In 2001, Per became one of the first employees to join Robert's team, and became responsible for bringing LEGO SERIOUS PLAY to the European markets. Together we also formed the master trainer team for the LEGO SERIOUS PLAY certification program. Between 2001 and the end of 2003, the Executive Discovery team consisted of up to 10 very different and highly dedicated people located in Connecticut and Tennessee (United States); Milan, Italy; and Munich, Germany.

Looking back, we realize that we were blessed with a certain naïveté. We truly believed that the world was open and ready for our fantastic process. We decided to develop a partnership business model, where organizations would sign a partner contract once they had qualified and had completed Executive Discovery's authorized facilitator training.

Choosing a partner model with authorized facilitators was a result of our early failed experiments. The value in the method does not come from the LEGO bricks, but rather from the combination of the bricks and the facilitation of the process. The model made it possible for us to control who had access to the intellectual property and to the accompanying kits. The first facilitators were trained in September 2001, and in January 2002 LEGO SERIOUS PLAY was officially launched with the revised facilitator training.

At the end of 2003, the LEGO SERIOUS PLAY idea faced its second existential crisis. The idea had not taken off globally as anticipated. There were bright spots and success stories, but overall, we were far from reaching our aspirations.

Though the method lived up to our expectations, marketing and selling the idea were much harder than anyone had expected. The media coverage showed us that it would be almost impossible to shed the toy image. The business setup proved to be too expensive and the company structure inappropriate. Combined with the discovery of financial skeletons in the closet dating back to the early days of the venture, Executive Discovery ceased to exist by end of December 2003. The team was dissolved, the LEGO Company acquired all the intellectual property (IP), and the cooperation with Johan Roos and Bart Victor was terminated.

In the beginning of 2004 the LEGO Company itself was at the peak of its crisis and fighting for its own survival. In this climate there was little interest in doing anything with the LEGO SERIOUS PLAY idea. Fortunately, the initiative has had several dedicated ambassadors inside the company throughout its life without whom it would not be alive today. These individuals came to its rescue and secured the establishment of a LEGO SERIOUS PLAY business line inside the company with the necessary resources for continued development and distribution. Per assumed the role of director of the business line working from his base in Milan, while Robert started building his own LEGO SERIOUS PLAY business in the United States.

Per's first task back at LEGO was to rethink the business model and revise the documentation material and the training format. In addition, he set out to prove the business he was asked to deliver on both bottom line and top line. He had until the end of 2004 to do this.

Alas, one of the first consequences of returning to the LEGO Company was that the original partner model was developed into a license fee-based model. This was done to supplement the revenue generated by the sales of the special LEGO SERIOUS PLAY kits that still could be purchased only with a valid partner and license contract with LEGO.

The business aspiration was to grow organically with a keen eye on the cost. The mantra was to keep it alive, keep it growing, and do so with the lowest possible cost and investments. The targets were met, and LEGO SERIOUS PLAY seemed to head into reasonably calm waters. In late 2005 Per left to join a leadership position outside the LEGO Group. However, he remained associated with LEGO SERIOUS PLAY through a position on an advisory board and, together with Robert, also continued to deliver facilitator training on behalf of LEGO.

Business remained steady up to 2007. It was maintenance of the idea and slow growth, but ideas were emerging that this could only be a temporary approach; something had to happen. Two options for the future were discussed; it was time to either give up or gear up. Around 2007, the choice fell on the latter and the individuals responsible for the LEGO SERIOUS PLAY business line began developing their new strategy. This fork in the road was the third existential crisis.

The goal was to implement a strategy that could create enough revenue to afford a larger dedicated team within the company and further development of the business. The chosen strategy was two-pronged: grow the partner business by appointing a lead partner within each geographical region, and develop internal competences to deliver the service to end customers—that is, develop a LEGO SERIOUS PLAY consultancy service.

The plan looked good on paper, and was launched in 2007. A new leader was hired for the business, who began building the internal team and preparing the rollout of the new strategy in 2008. Robert became part of this new team. In early 2008, he and his family moved back to Denmark and joined the LEGO SERIOUS PLAY team part-time while continuing his LEGO SERIOUS PLAY business in the United States. His responsibility was to train facilitators and investigate the development of new applications. Per became a member of the newly formed partner council and functioned at times as an external resource to the team.

Things were becoming increasingly unstable by 2008; the team as a whole proved to have limited understanding of LEGO SERIOUS PLAY and for the LEGO culture and leadership. Eventually, by the end of the year, Robert saw no other opportunity than to leave LEGO and the LEGO SERIOUS PLAY team. Then in early 2009, just as implementation was getting off the ground, the new leader was fired—thereby putting the new growth and gear-up strategy on hold and bringing LEGO SERIOUS PLAY to its fourth existential crisis. Since 2002 there had been a growing community of LEGO SERIOUS PLAY practitioners, whose main concern was figuring out how to continue their business with the method. Part of this was getting access to purchasing the special LEGO SERIOUS PLAY kits produced and distributed by the LEGO Company.

In May 2010, LEGO was ready to announce its new strategy to the LEGO SERIOUS PLAY community. It was not *give up* or *gear up* this time, however; it was *grow up*! Ever since the business model's launch in 2002, the assumption had been that LEGO had to be in full control of who they would train, certify, and give the rights to deliver the services to the end customers. It was assumed that unless this process was under the complete control of LEGO, the risk of damaging the brand experience and becoming a fad simply was too high.

The "grow-up" strategy made access to using the methodology more akin to open source; it became known as the community model. Gone were the requirements for a LEGO-delivered certification training, or for a partner and license contract with LEGO in order to be able to purchase the special LEGO SERIOUS PLAY kits. LEGO decided to give this strategy a two-year trial period, hoping that the concept now was so well known that the easier accessibility would lead to significant growth and that the established community would be strong enough to still secure a use that was consistent with the method's core values. This approach would allow the LEGO Company to reduce its involvement to supplying the LEGO SERIOUS PLAY materials and support to the community with a dedicated website (www.seriousplay.com) only, and an annual conference focusing on sharing best practice.

When the trial period ended in mid-2012, the conclusion from both inside and outside the LEGO Company was unanimous: LEGO SERIOUS PLAY and its community of believers and practitioners had actually grown up. They lived up to the expectations of maintaining the quality of the brand and the delivery. As a result, the LEGO Company committed to keeping the LEGO SERIOUS PLAY brand alive in the future. It also accepted that the main reasons for doing so should not be dictated purely by the commercial bottom-line results for the business line. As a consequence, the responsibility for the business line was transferred partly to the LEGO Foundation, a not-for-profit foundation founded by the Kirk Kristiansen family and associated with the LEGO Company.

Who is this grown-up community of LEGO SERIOUS PLAY facilitators, some of whom have been committed to the process since the very beginning? It is a highly diverse group that comes from almost every corner of the world. The method has proven to work equally well in Europe, Asia, the Americas, Africa, and the Middle East, across cultures and in any language. The principles and techniques forming the method seem to be highly universal.

You might be prompted to ask: how can a thinking, communication, and problem-solving methodology like LEGO SERIOUS PLAY, developed more than 10 years ago, still be relevant and appropriate today in its same form? But in fact, it may be even *more* attractive than when this journey began! Think about it: although a 10-year-old car still fulfills the basic requirements for being able to transport you from A to B, it would not be especially appealing nowadays. Cars from both decades have the same basic components: four wheels, an engine, seats, and a steering wheel. But compared to an automobile from 2003, a 2013 model has much better fuel economy and safety, is more comfortable to ride in, has a sleeker design, and has a GPS so that it always knows where it is.

This would be an apt metaphor for LEGO SERIOUS PLAY. From afar, the method looks the same and has those consistent fundamental components. Yet it is significantly more sophisticated today than when launched in 2002. It has better fuel economy—that is, more value delivered in less time. The driving experience is faster; that is, the applications are more targeted. And the information from the instrument panel to the driver—the design—has been vastly expanded. The facilitation of the application processes is now based on understanding of the science of LEGO SERIOUS PLAY, instead of intuition and assumptions as it was in the original development phase.

Staying with the car metaphor, one could say that LEGO SERIOUS PLAY in 2002 was like the Model T Ford; that is, you could have it any color you wanted as long as it was black. In 2014, it has all the qualities mentioned previously. While it is still a vehicle whose job is to get you from point A to point B, you can now have it in many versions, and, importantly, you can have it customized to serve your unique needs.

Raising LEGO SERIOUS PLAY from its inception to its teenage years has been a true "hard fun" journey, one with many ups and also quite a few downs. It still is. What gives it the fun is the payoff—not in terms of money but in terms of the insight and experience, on both a business level and a personal level, that process users have gained.

Over the next 15 chapters, we invite you to travel with us through the world of LEGO SERIOUS PLAY. We will take you through the science-platform, why and how it works, its applications, and where has it worked and on what problems; and finally, we will share some of the aspirations for its continued development. We'll begin with Part I, The LEGO SERIOUS PLAY Territory, which looks at why the method exists and what are the key elements.

Over the years, many people have described their insights from using the LEGO SERIOUS PLAY methodology as a life-changing experience.

This book may not be quite as life-changing an experience for you as a reader; but then again, anything's possible. Enjoy!

The LEGO® SERIOUS PLAY® Territory

This part will map the landscape, or as we have chosen to call it, the *territory* of LEGO SERIOUS PLAY. We will cover four areas that are essential for understanding the method, and specifically discuss:

1. The business needs for which the method provides a great solution, and the challenges that the method evolved to deal with
2. What the LEGO brick is, the power behind it, its history, how it is used in LEGO SERIOUS PLAY, and the difference it makes
3. What we mean by the term *serious play*
4. How all of this comes together in what we define as the LEGO SERIOUS PLAY method

CHAPTER 1
The Need for Building Better Businesses

The book's Introduction provided information on how the LEGO® SERIOUS PLAY® method was developed to specifically address challenges that LEGO faced. Though many things have changed since the turn of 2001/2002, challenges like these have only become even clearer and more urgent. Our experience has brought to light a number of issues in how business and management is conducted that have led to a continued demand or need for LEGO SERIOUS PLAY, and the difference it can make.

Three areas where LEGO SERIOUS PLAY provides a solution are:

1. Beyond 20/80 meetings and Creating leaning in
2. Leading to unlock
3. Breaking habitual thinking

We present this sequence (as shown in Figure 1.1) in this particular order for a reason: first the manager has to break the 20/80 dynamics and create meetings where everybody is leaning in and contributing. Once this happens, he or she needs to lead to unlock everyone's full potential and, finally, do so in a way that breaks the habitual thinking and unearths new and surprising insights.

Our description of the *types* of challenges focuses less on the content and more on dynamics or structure. This aligns with our view of LEGO SERIOUS PLAY as a *language*. The manager may want to go beyond 20/80, lead to unlock, or break habitual thinking on almost any complex issue.

So, let's go into a bit more depth on the three types of challenges.

FIGURE 1.1   How the Method Creates Value

BEYOND 20/80 AND CREATING LEANING IN

The drawing in Figure 1.2 captures the flow, or lack of flow, of most meetings in many organizations.

One or two individuals, often the most senior member and/or the meeting's host, control and enjoy the meeting. These 20 percent of the participants take 80 percent of the time, hence the title of 20/80. To make matters worse, these individuals typically contribute only 70 to 80 percent of their full potential in order to solve the meeting's issues. The remaining 80 percent of the participants contribute far less, arguably down to a few percent of their potential. In addition, they have a negative experience—a feeling that they may even carry into work *after* the meeting.

The main reason for this is that a couple of such dominant, extroverted or quick-thinking people around the table immediately start talking, prompting them to take over the agenda and the angle from which the content is discussed. There is no democratic process ensuring that everybody both has a voice and is obliged to use it.

These meetings very often have an additional characteristic: the participants are *physically leaning out* rather than *leaning into* the conversation. They push away from the table, slide down into their chairs, glance out the window, or check e-mails or

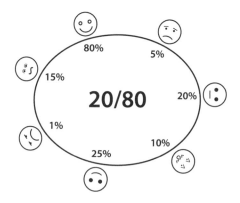

FIGURE 1.2   Typical 20/80 Meeting

status on social media on their smartphones. Their bodily actions mirror their state of mind, and highlight their rather unengaged position.

Both 20/80 and leaning out are dynamics that lead to lower-quality in-person meetings. The so-called attention density is low. We will refer to attention density further in Chapter 7; however, the key definition of it is that it is the combination of *how long* we pay attention to something and *how much* we pay attention to it. The *how much* can further be divided into are we listening, or are we listening and looking, or are we even listening, looking, and touching. Meeting attendees are creating very little or even no new knowledge, and thus no new solutions. These meetings may even destroy value—partly because the participants are taken away from value-creating activities, partly because employees haven't solved the complex issue the meeting was intended to address, and partly because the meeting itself destroys collaborative efforts between the individuals and may even create stress (which has a very negative impact on the brain).

Managers and leaders need to create 100/100 meetings, conversations where 100 percent of attendees are contributing their full potential—100 percent of what they have to offer.

LEADING IN ORDER TO UNLOCK

Once the manager has succeeded in creating 100/100 meetings where all participants contribute, a new leadership challenge emerges: leading to *unlock*.

Specifically, managers must unlock potential in three areas: the knowledge in the room, people's understanding of the system, and the connection between the individual's and the organization's purpose. Let's look at each of these.

The Knowledge in the Room

Knowledge is the first area where the manager's role will change. We all have access to more data and information nowadays than any one person can handle, or even has the remotest chance of remembering. Very often, we aren't even aware of or certain about our own knowledge on a given topic. Therefore, when you have a number of very smart people suddenly eager to contribute but who don't necessarily know exactly *how* they can form a solution, it becomes the leader/manager's job to unlock each individual's knowledge and uncover patterns in what each is sharing.

We have just indicated an interesting angle that makes this challenge even more daunting: people themselves often *don't even know what they know*. This has to do with the intricacies of our brains; part of what we know is stored deeply in the brain but other elements are stored in different places in the cortex or even the hippocampus. And since we don't always know exactly how much we know, we're frequently not even aware that we know something.

Chapter 7 will go into more detail on memory. For now, the message is this: in order to innovate and transform businesses and activities, everyone needs to activate more of their knowledge and find underlying and often surprising patterns. Additionally, if we want to intentionally transform an activity—individually or as team—we need to make this clear and shared. And leading to unlock requires us to make this possible.

Understanding the System

The manager's second task is to help unlock the understanding or *properties* of the system. This includes creating a culture and process where there is an understanding that the organization needs to probe, sense, and then respond—and doing so in a sustainable manner. This need has become more urgent recently, since most of today's organizations compete or collaborate in complex adaptive systems. Unlocking this understanding is crucial, because complex adaptive systems have emergent properties. When a system has emergent properties, it means that we cannot predict or outline how a single alteration may change the entire system. Such alterations, often called emergence, are defined by being dynamic, unforeseen, and changing the state of the system.

The leadership challenge has moved from succeeding in the simple systems of years gone by, and in most cases also beyond succeeding in complicated systems. In simple systems, it was possible to make sense of information, categorize, and respond accordingly. Best practices worked, and bureaucracies excelled in such systems.

Though this is a bit more challenging in complicated systems, they still offer the opportunity to make sense of information. Individuals can then analyze and respond based on this understanding. Experts fare well in complicated systems; one could ponder whether the "manager as an expert" paradigm is a natural response to competing in a complicated system.

However, a complex system takes on emergent properties. Consequently, managers and employees cannot collect the information in an inactive manner. Rather, they have to probe the system, learn from this, and *then* respond. There is more mutual influence here; agents coevolve the system, which is why understanding has to be unlocked.

This process includes developing an understanding of the group's current identity, what it can be in the future, and how this would change the system. We can perceive the identity as a strange attractor in the complex adaptive system. It also requires that members of a group get a grasp on what they can change versus what they cannot, and in which combinations. Finally, all of this must be monitored.

Connecting Purposes between Organization and Individual

Finally, the manager is left with the *unlocking the connection* between the purpose of the company and the employees. This element in some part builds directly on what happens when the group is able to unlock an understanding of the system. As written earlier, this is based on the ability to understand the group's identity, which inevitably leads to a clarification of its purpose.

When a manager is able to create a connection between the organization's and the employees' purposes, then engagement typically grows; the organization fares better, and the employees are more satisfied. Connecting purposes creates similar pursuits and more meaningful relationships between all parties involved, and benefits everyone—including the customer.

Many make the argument that members of the workforce are increasingly fickle or substantially more loyal to their personal life vision rather than that of the company. Hence, if a company can connect its own goals with its employees' goals, the organization becomes more resilient and more agile at a time when those capabilities are needed most.

BREAKING HABITUAL THINKING

As mentioned earlier in this chapter, employees have access to a lot of data, and often have a very deep understanding of their expertise. While this occasionally leads to the challenge of unlocking all of this knowledge, it also brings to light another challenge: breaking habitual thinking.

We humans tend to look for the first pattern that fits what we know, and then stay with it. A strong subject matter expertise often leads us to feel that we know what to look for, and hence will look *only for that*. We will find data that support us and, unfortunately, unconsciously ignore disturbing information. This causes us to miss surprising and valuable patterns.

We see a classic example of this in Christopher Chabris and Daniel Simons's *The Invisible Gorilla* test, where they studied the concept of selective attention.[1] In this experiment, the observer sees two teams of young people standing in a circle and passing two basketballs between them. The observer is then challenged to count how often one of the teams passes the ball. Midway through the video an adult dressed up like a gorilla goes into the middle of the circle, punches its chest, and seemingly roars. Very few people see the gorilla, for the simple reason that they are focused on counting passes. It is very likely that such selective focus was part of the downfall of Kodak, as it kept ignoring digital photography, or Blockbuster missing out on streaming, unlike its then competitor Netflix. However, this is not a recent phenomenon; in 1878 Sir William Preece, chief engineer at the British Post Office, said:

> The Americans have need of the telephone, but we do not. We have plenty of messenger boys.

Clearly the wrong data to focus on.

Therefore, the manager's final challenge is to help the team members to break their habitual patterns of thinking. He or she needs to help everyone suspend going for the first acceptable solution, and instead think once more, think differently, and then see the new pattern that leads to a surprising solution. Here is an example of how this worked out for the manager and founder of Scurri, an Internet start-up based on the coast of Ireland.

Case Example: Developing a Business Model at an Internet Start-Up

Background: Scurri, an Internet start-up, was a couple of years into its existence; it had successfully raised capital twice, and a good team had been assembled. The company worked to Eric Ries's Lean Start-Up philosophy, used the Lean Canvas (Ash Maurya) for its product focus, and in addition used Alexander Osterwalder's Business Model Canvas for more strategic discussions.

Issue: To accelerate Scurri's growth, the founder and CEO felt that the team had to understand the entire business model, and how the elements impacted each other.

LEGO SERIOUS PLAY intervention: The entire team of seven people gathered for a long day. The workshop was designed based on the Business Model Canvas. The team explored the key activities, key resources, value proposition, partners, and customer segments. All of it was placed in a landscape closely mirroring the canvas.

Outcome: Based on the workshop, Scurri redefined its value proposition, chose two new customer segments to focus on, and identified the key partners that could help leverage this new focus. Everything was captured in a "Business Model Wiki," which became an operational tool for the team. Scurri has now successfully expanded into the United Kingdom, has raised more capital, is forecasted to be one of Ireland's top 10 Internet start-ups for 2014, and is growing substantially.

CONTEMPLATING THE NEEDS

The red thread through all the needs that we have listed here is that the manager wants—truly, needs—to build a better and more sustainable business. However, he or she must do it by unlocking something so far unknown. These unknowns are knowledge both within each person's head and between people's brains, knowledge of the system, the connection between purposes, and finding the surprise by breaking habitual thinking.

Once the manager uses the LEGO SERIOUS PLAY method to unlock these unknowns, he or she can create a deep impact where the transformation happens on two levels:

1. Individually, for the employees involved in the workshop, it changes something in their understanding and thus their personal commitment to change.
2. Organizationally, it changes how the organization works. This could, for example, be in the direction (vision) or in how decisions are made between people (culture).

Are these challenges new? Are they unique to the time we live in? Maybe not, as always, change has never happened faster than "right now." The following is a classic quote attributed to *Scientific American* in 1867:

It is not too much to say. . . that more has been done, richer and more prolific discoveries have been made, grander achievements have been realized in the course of the 50 years of our own lifetime than in all the previous lifetime of the race. It is in the three momentous matters of light, locomotion, and communication that the progress effected in this generation contrasts surprisingly with the aggregate of the progress effected in all the generations put together since the earliest dawn of authentic history.

If nothing else, it is a good reminder that everyone has always lived in times of great change, and it has never happened faster than whenever "right now" may be.

Consequently, managers have always been met with increasingly difficult problems, shorter development time, higher pace of change, and so on.

It's important to consider what characterizes the system and the time in which these complex problems arise. We see the need for LEGO SERIOUS PLAY tying to a period where everyone has real-time access to abundant data and information, but struggle with making sense of it, let alone connecting individual knowledge to shared knowledge.

In addition, there is a growing need to balance two different but possibly complementary forces: high tech and high touch. We are entering an age where both forces are simultaneously at play. High tech offers a range of virtual solutions to human interaction, from relative simple time/place independent idea generation to virtual reality. Parallel to this, many individuals and organizations are deliberately choosing to focus on the concrete in-person experience of an interaction, aiming to strengthen that interaction's attention density.

We see a balance forming: though there are more virtual interactions and fewer in-person interactions, the demanded outcome of the in-person meetings will be higher than what is often expected today. Attention density has to be high, and there will be a code of conduct stressing that those in the room are immersed in the interaction.

And this demand for the quality of the high-touch meeting is creating three essential needs for which LEGO SERIOUS PLAY works well. You've probably guessed them: going beyond 20/80 meetings, leading in order to unlock knowledge, and the need to break habitual thinking.

The method is designed to counter these challenges and provide added value in terms of enhanced insights, confidence, and commitment. It does this through a unique facilitation approach—a specific set of group dynamics and learning sciences. In this way, it creates a language that connects within and between brains. An essential and very concrete element in that language is the LEGO brick, and the particular way it is used in LEGO SERIOUS PLAY.

CHAPTER 2
The LEGO® Brick

In the LEGO® SERIOUS PLAY® method, participants answer a series of questions that delve a bit deeper with each step. Each participant builds his or her own three-dimensional LEGO model in response to these questions by using specially selected LEGO bricks. These 3-D models serve as the basis for group discussion, knowledge sharing, problem solving, and decision making. Without the LEGO brick, there is no LEGO SERIOUS PLAY method.

The quintessential LEGO brick is the 4 × 2 red stud brick shown in Figure 2.1.

Eight of these bricks can be combined in 915,103,765 ways.

Children and adults have used this brick and millions of others to build models of their world for about 60 years. They've used them to create pieces of the real world they saw and the one they imagined. Additionally, plenty of parents have accidently stepped on these bricks over the years and let out a sound of sheer pain (perhaps even a profanity or two).

The LEGO brick's history begins in 1949, when company founder Ole Kirk Christiansen and his son Godtfred Kirk Christiansen modified British inventor Hilary Fisher Pag's "Self-Locking Building Bricks." Pag's bricks had two rows of four studs that children could use to build small houses and other creations. The Christiansens' modification was quite minor, and they named their new brick the "Automatic Binding Brick." It looked very similar to the bricks we know today on the top, but it was hollow underneath.

FIGURE 2.1   LEGO 4 × 2 Stud Brick

One significant difference between a 1949 brick and a 2014 brick is that the early bricks did not click together; users merely stacked them on top of each other. As a result, the structures that children built fell apart fairly easily—and building a slanted roof overlapping the bricks was impossible. It took LEGO the better part of a decade and thousands of experiments before it patented the design in 1958 that made the LEGO Company what it is today.

The official LEGO term for the bricks' clicking together feature is *clutch power*. As explained by David Robertson in his 2013 book *Brick by Brick*, "Born out of a seemingly unending series of experiments more than half a century ago, it is clutch power that makes LEGO such an endlessly expandable toy, one that lets kids build whatever they imagine. And it is the brick that became the physical manifestation of an entire philosophy about learning through play."[1]

Godtfred Kirk Christiansen took over the LEGO Company in 1950. History has it that the idea for a true system came from a conversation with the manager of a toy store in a leading shopping center in Copenhagen. Certainly, Christiansen saw early on the potential in the endless play possibilities that a modular play system would give children. His vision was to create a toy that prepares the child for life.

Appealing to the imagination and developing the creative urge and joy of creating are the driving forces in every human being. Christiansen already understood then that the creative urge and joy of creating are not something you ever outgrow. They remain with you, and through LEGO SERIOUS PLAY adults today have the opportunity to feel and nurture this joy.

Godtfred Kirk Christiansen formulated a set of guiding principles to ensure that future generations would constantly keep the values he established alive. These principles guided the development of the new products, and stated that LEGO's offerings must always be:

- Limited in size without setting limitations for imagination
- Affordable
- Simple, durable, and offering rich variations

- For girls, for boys, and fun at every age
- A classic among toys, without the need for renewal
- Easy to distribute[2]

At the beginning of the 1960s, the LEGO Company embarked on a growth curve that extended its reach—through western Europe and on into the United States, Asia, Australia, and South America—and also expanded its range of game-changing products throughout the course of that decade. Among the highlights were the 1961 invention of the (LEGO) wheel, a round brick with a rubber tire that LEGO produces some three hundred million of annually today. In 1967, LEGO unveiled the DUPLO brick, a line of bigger bricks for little hands. Then, in 1968, the first LEGOLAND theme park opened in Billund, Denmark.

In 1979 Kjeld Kirk Kristiansen took over as CEO of the company after his father Godtfred. Over the next 15 years, he led the company's extraordinary expansion, doubling in size every five years. This remarkable growth came as a result of Kirk Kristiansen realizing his visions, including a huge expansion of the DUPLO range, a complete redesign of the "LEGO System of Play" that included the LEGO Minifigure, and an emphasis on the notion of themed sets to make children's play experience more rewarding. One result of this focus on theme was two of the company's greatest successes, Castle and Space.

Since the launch of the first LEGO theme set in 1955, countless sets and themes have followed. All of them have inspired children to build models of the real world (towns, castles, ships, fire stations, spacecraft, airplanes, etc.) or an imaginary world (e.g., *Star Wars*, Bionicles, or Harry Potter). As one of the company's 1960s ad campaigns proclaimed, whatever you built with LEGO bricks is always "real as real."

USING THE LEGO BRICK OUTSIDE THE PLAYROOM

The LEGO vision for the LEGO brick is that it is "more than a toy." It is a language for systematic creativity.

This notion has been part of propelling the brick into many applications for learning and business. The educational division of LEGO has a long and robust history in using the bricks as vehicles for learning science, math, technology, and engineering in primary and secondary school and educational systems all over the world.

For example, one well-known product from LEGO Education is the LEGO Mindstorms, where both children and adults program a robot to do anything from finding its way through a complex maze to playing chess with its builder.

LEGO Architecture sets allow adults to build scale models of famous buildings such as the Sears Tower and Falling Water. In the business world, designers use

FIGURE 2.2   LEGO Motorcycle—Classic Use of the LEGO Brick

LEGO bricks for rapid prototyping, simulations, and visualizations. Consultants use LEGO bricks for team building, modeling of factories, and logistic processes.

What is common for both the classic "real as real" use of the LEGO brick and its use for learning and business is that the bricks are used as stand-ins. The models that people build—machines, robots, prototypes, buildings, chess games—are meant to represent or to visualize something tangible, whether a given product or a supply chain. The model or the process of building should resemble or mirror the real-world topic as much as possible. In doing so, you are using the LEGO brick as a metonym—"a figure of speech consisting of the use of the name of one thing for that of another of which it is an attribute or with which it is associated" (Merriam-Webster). The classic use of the LEGO brick is to build models or representations of the tangible world. Figure 2.2 is an image of a LEGO motorcycle. The more it looks like an actual motorcycle, the better it is.

THE LEGO SERIOUS PLAY USE OF THE LEGO BRICK

Contrary to the classic use of the LEGO brick to build models of the tangible world, the brick in LEGO SERIOUS PLAY is used to build stories about the intangible world. They allow us to form concrete 3-D models about things that are not physically concrete.

The focus in LEGO SERIOUS PLAY is not on the bricks; it is on the story they create. Yet there is no story without the bricks. The bricks and the models become metaphors, and the landscapes of the models become stories.

The two different uses of the LEGO brick are illustrated in Figures 2.3 and 2.4. To the left it is used as a metonym and to the right it is used as a metaphor for a manager who behaves like crocodile and has a poisonous tongue.

The story-making and subsequent storytelling that the method makes possible use the metaphor—that is, a form of thinking and language through which we understand or experience one thing in terms of another. Merriam-Webster defines a metaphor as "a form of expression used to convey meaning or heighten effect often by comparing

FIGURE 2.3   A Crocodile   **FIGURE 2.4   An Unpleasant Manager**

or identifying one thing with another that has a meaning or connotation familiar to the reader or listener." Metaphor is a type of analogy that compares two objects or things without using the words *like* or *as* and achieves their effects via association, comparison, or resemblance; it typically also allows one of the objects to borrow qualities from another object.

This more elaborate use of the bricks as metaphors describes the identity of a research and development (R&D) group shown in Figure 2.5. The skeletons represent their willingness to give up ideas, the dog shows that they feel like underdogs in relation to other departments, the man walking out on the edge to the left shows their willingness to take risks, the cow in front illustrates the group's ability to deliver, and the construction on the top illustrates that the users of the products they develop are children.

Each LEGO piece or combination of pieces has a meaning.

In his 1971 book *Beyond the Stable State*, Massachusetts Institute of Technology (MIT) professor Donald Schön has argued that metaphors can actually generate

FIGURE 2.5   An Organization's Identity

radically new ways of understanding things.[3] He observed how when trying to make an artificial bristle paintbrush, product development researchers had a breakthrough when one member of the group observed, "A paintbrush is a kind of pump." According to Schön, metaphor is much more than just "flowery language"; it can play an active, constructive, and creative role in human cognition. Metaphors provide richer descriptions of our realities that might challenge assumptions and reveal new possibilities.

The link between metaphors and learning has been widely researched. Metaphors generate radically new ways of understanding things.[4] A series of dominant metaphors shape the way we understand organizations in which we work.[5] Metaphors transform us in their potential to uncover perceptions, attitudes, and feelings that were previously subconscious or unarticulated.

THE LEGO SERIOUS PLAY KITS

"Can I take some of these bricks home to my children? They would love some of these pieces." "I didn't know LEGO had this kind of bricks." These are just two of the comments we hear from the participants in a LEGO SERIOUS PLAY workshop. LEGO has never produced any special bricks for LEGO SERIOUS PLAY and will probably never have to do so, either.

The sets produced for LEGO SERIOUS PLAY are merely collections of standard LEGO bricks. However, the mix is unique compared to the normal boxes from LEGO, as well as those from LEGO Education. The latter are highly specialized to allow participants to build the models following the instructions in the sets.

There are no instructions in a LEGO SERIOUS PLAY set, and the mix of elements represents the full range of available LEGO bricks—from basic DUPLO and DUPLO animals to LEGO Technic gear wheels and everything in between. As illustrated in the large metaphor example in Figure 2.5, the bricks' enhanced diversity allows more meaning to be expressed in the workshop.

Workshop participants often ask whether people with LEGO building experience or expertise have a particular advantage when engaging in LEGO SERIOUS PLAY versus those who have never played with LEGO bricks before. Based on 10 years of experience, our answer is an emphatic "No!" In fact, we often see that extensive LEGO building expertise can be a *disadvantage* for some. How does this work? Well, many inexperienced builders tend to fear that this is about building elaborate and intricate LEGO models. However, when they realize that the experience is not about the model but rather about the meaning and story in the model, they relax and are often able to produce creations that are more direct and to the point. Sophisticated builders sometimes come up short; they are so focused on the material that they forget the meaning, or are so accustomed to using the LEGO materials for building models to represent something tangible that it is almost impossible for them to see a red 2 × 4 brick as "passion" or "love." People who think of themselves as creative and/or architects often run into the same issue.

One of the LEGO bricks' most significant features is the fact that you can take them apart and start over, and they will work as if they were brand-new. This makes using the LEGO bricks for creating and cocreating metaphors and stories superior to practically any other hands-on material.

The LEGO SERIOUS PLAY method is open-ended, yet takes place within a system that makes constructing both fast and forgiving. If you do not like what you have built, you simply take it apart and build something else. And while you could use clay, pipe cleaners, Popsicle sticks, or some other cheaper material, it would never be able to match the LEGO bricks' variety, speed, forgiveness, and accessibility for all, regardless of prior experience with the LEGO materials. You could also ask people to draw metaphors and stories instead. That would work for young children, who still think of themselves as artists. However, it would likely be more difficult with adults since we have been conditioned into clear expectations about what things should look like; we get caught up in the details of the representation, whether the proportions are correct, whether it looks like an elephant, and so on. And, in addition, to most adults, the proverbial blank sheet is not liberating; it is limiting. It puts us out of flow, as we do not know where to begin. We no longer consider ourselves artists, and therefore we do not feel proud of the result, as we do with a LEGO construction. Ultimately, adults in most cases do get something on paper since they feel committed to do so. However, the results vary so much from individual to individual that the communicative value is highly limited.

Without the bricks, there is no LEGO SERIOUS PLAY method. The LEGO bricks are, however, only the means to get people to lean forward, unlock knowledge, and break habitual thinking. The end is reached through the concept of serious play. In the next chapter we will define serious play and look into why we as adults engage in serious play, how we do it, and how this helps build better businesses.

CHAPTER 3
Defining Serious Play

The next important habitat in the LEGO® SERIOUS PLAY® territory is play—but not just any play, serious play. This kind of play has an explicit purpose and is done in a particular way. This chapter provides an explanation of what we mean by this kind of play. We'll give examples of play with a purpose and define what we mean by serious play.

The first thing we must carve in stone is that serious play is "play with an explicit purpose." That purpose is to address a real issue for the participants around the table by getting them to lean forward, unlock knowledge, and break habitual thinking.

It is not frivolous play; it is not taking a break from work, and it is something subtly different from many other important kinds of play in which lots of learning also is involved (for more on play, different kinds of play, and ways of categorizing them, see Chapter 10).

INTRODUCTION TO PLAY

We should probably make it clear that *most* play is anything but frivolous. Even the kinds in which we partake when we're young typically have some sort of developmental purpose, even though this purpose typically is not explicitly stated.

The implicit developmental purposes of play are as numerous as its subcategories. We are not going to go into all of these here. What is far more helpful is for us to present how Johan Huizinga in his groundbreaking book *Homo Ludens* defined what play is and what it does for children: "An activity is playful if it is: 1. Fully absorbing, 2. Intrinsically motivated, 3. Includes elements of uncertainty, or surprise, and 4. If it involves a sense of illusion or exaggeration." Huizinga explains, "Play comes from an innate propensity to imitate, to relieve accumulated stress, or to prepare and exercise for more serious functional actions."[1] Examples here could be a child building with LEGO bricks; the child is typically fully absorbed and intrinsically motivated to build something, possibly reflecting a personal experience; the uncertainty could be related to if or how it will be possible to complete the construction; and often LEGO construction exaggerates the qualities of what it is meant to represent, and/or it is an illusion as it represents an imaginary world (e.g., where the child is a farmer).[2]

Dr. Stuart Brown, the founder and head of the National Institute for Play, Carmel Valley, California, makes this point as well: "Play is our natural way of adapting and developing new skills. It is what prepares us for emergence, and keeps us open to serendipity, to new opportunities. It prepares us for ambiguity."[3] Thus, play is our natural response; it helps us adapt and become resilient, and keeps us open to new opportunities—exactly the same qualities one would want to bring to the boardroom.

Clearly, there is more involved in the process of play. And while children's play is an important developmental activity, children do not explicitly *choose* play to develop their skills, their competencies, or solutions to a challenge that they are facing. They're simply doing it to have fun, and because it comes so naturally to them. But does it come as naturally to adults? We will return to play in Chapter 10, but for now we will use this short outline as a stepping-stone into the concept of serious play. We will later, in Chapter 10, take up this thread again.

SERIOUS PLAY DEFINED

Progressing from the broader sense of play via playing with a purpose, we define serious play by three key characteristics:

1. It is an intentional gathering to apply the imagination.
2. It is exploring and preparing, not implementing.
3. It follows a specific set of rules or language.

Intentional Gathering to Apply the Imagination

Participants plan the meeting and mutually agree that its purpose is to apply their imaginations to a real issue in order to develop a solution. It might be to an existing problem, or it could be a desired new state; so the goal is to close either a performance gap or an opportunity gap.

The participants know that they will be engaging their imaginations—that is, their ability to form a mental image of something that does not yet exist—in order to see things that have not happened yet. They're exploring a possible and plausible state or seeing the current reality in a different way and understanding its complexity and uncertainty in a different way.

They may deliberately do this to challenge and undo what is or simply to form a new and shared understanding.

This characteristic is clearly seen in, for example, scenario development.

Exploring and Preparing, Not Implementing

The participants are free to imagine many different things during the play process. They explore different paths, zigzag, and find what does and does not work. Many of the things that are proposed will remain merely ideas; others will be carried into action. But action isn't the point of the process; imagining is.

The participants engage in play in order to learn, generate options, and develop new understandings together. A serious play process may lead to a new vision or a business model. To achieve this, participants explore many versions. They end up with one shared model by the end of the play—the model that will guide them in making decisions about who to partner with, how to make investments, and other details about what steps to take going forward. This was, for example, what happened for Scurri, the Irish Internet start-up in Chapter 1 that used its results from a Business Model Canvas workshop to focus on a new customer segment, and to work with a different group of partners to reach that segment. In that chapter, we also mentioned how most organizations compete in complex adaptive systems, and that these are unpredictable and can be understood only by observing how they respond to events. The process of playing seriously can help do this; it makes it possible for the participants to play out events in their landscape, which is a play version of probing their complex adaptive system, thereby making it possible to make sense of the system.

Therefore, the value is partly in the process that led the participants to it, and partly in how it prepares the participants for making better decisions. It gives them guidance and direction, sometimes opening up new paths to explore.

We can clearly see this characteristic in war games. Obviously, participants are not directly engaged in a war; so in terms of war and/or security being their product, they are not implementing the war activities. But they are *undertaking a process* that prepares them for making better decisions, that aligns their goals and action points, and that creates new learning. Similarly, the architects are not actually building the house; they are exploring what it could look like, how the people who live in it could interact with it, and what materials would be best to build it.

We can also apply a metaphor inspired by physics to explain this: the purpose of serious play is to create *potential* energy. This then becomes kinetic energy when the team members implement it—when they literally put it to work. Serious play generates the kind of energy that has a significant impact on a person, team, or organization when goals are realized. But one can create this potential energy only if the process is real, it is intensive, and it involves the right organizational issue.

Hence, when decisions are made, the group must explicitly agree to make decisions when it is time to do so. This intentionality is one of the things that make serious play distinct from children's play. It is also what makes serious play risk free. It creates the time and space in which employees can challenge strongly held beliefs and modi operandi that they might not otherwise be able to. It is therefore an essential element in breaking habitual thinking.

Specific Set of Rules or Language

When imagining, participants must follow a specific set of rules or language. This helps break the pattern of normal thinking and encourages participants to use their imaginations freely. They're able to immerse themselves in exploring possibilities rather than having to worry about making decisions. Most of us are conditioned to believe that we must make decisions as quickly and as early in the process as possible. Therefore, it takes a rather robust language system to break this, and help or even force the continued exploration and imagination phase.

This language helps create the space in which it is safe to imagine and *challenge*. The notion of the specific rules or language is very clear in the example of budgeting later in this chapter; similarly, there are clear rules and words to use when we create strategies or engage in war games. Strategy discussions, for example, may include terms like blue oceans, must-win battles, core competencies, and competitive advantage, and rules like a must-win battle has to "make a real difference," "be market focused," "create excitement," "be specific and tangible," and "be winnable"; and that before even looking at the must-win battle, one first has to "assess starting conditions" and "open windows." We will return to the specific rules of the LEGO SERIOUS PLAY method in Chapter 10.

The three characteristics listed on page 40 set serious play apart from work, and provide a clear distinction. The listed characteristics are also part of making serious play distinct from children's play. Nevertheless, play aficionados will undoubtedly find that the three characteristics are inspired by Roger Caillois.[4] We will return to serious play and children's play in Chapter 10.

Keeping this definition of serious play in mind, it should be clear that the LEGO SERIOUS PLAY method is not a training tool. One does not meet to imagine something that one of the participants already knows and only needs to convey to you.

Rather, LEGO SERIOUS PLAY is a thinking, communication, and problem-solving approach for topics that are real for the participants.

Play with a Purpose

When adults look to play as way to solve a specific developmental need, then it is meaningful to undertake play with a purpose. As mentioned, this purpose should be explicit and agreed upon between the participants before starting the play activity.

We see this kind of play often in organizations, a number of examples of which are outlined in the following pages. All of these examples have characteristics of serious play—not LEGO SERIOUS PLAY, but serious play as a play activity. Some of these examples might be surprising. We would argue that this is because the use of play has been challenged by conventional understandings of "work versus play" for a number of years.

The Army and War Games

Most armies in the world use elements of play, either when developing their soldiers or when cultivating war tactics and strategies prior to engaging in battle. Often different military interventions are played out before the individuals involved choose a final approach. Interestingly, the war room and the related vocabulary are widely used in business as metaphors. The war room is where the management team or a task force go to develop plans for "conquering new territory," "surviving in the market," or "winning"—that is, a place and activities that help the organization become better, not actually doing the actions.

Architects

Architects typically construct, test, and play with representations of the building or space they are creating.

Pilots

It is very hard to imagine anyone wanting to put a pilot in a plane without having him or her having built experience in a flight simulator. Such simulators help the pilots practice their flying and decision making in a playful and purposeful manner.

Strategy Making

Robust classic strategy making and strategy plans exhibit many traits of playing with a purpose. During the development process, participants imagine what markets they could potentially enter; what products, experiences, or propositions they might offer, and what each would cost; and how competitors, clients, and suppliers would respond.

Strictly speaking, the plan *itself* may not be part of the play. Rather, it's something one could almost see as the rule book that is generated based on what participants learn during the strategy-making process. This is one reason why companies and individuals must be nimble and willing to change plans regularly. For example, if your competitors respond in a completely different way than you imagined, then by definition the plan is also flawed—since everything that comes after this will play out differently. This relates to what President Eisenhower meant when he said that "Plans are nothing; planning is everything."

Scenario Planning/Development

In scenario development, participants meet to create narratives of a set of plausible futures, in order to use these to improve decision making. The narratives are typically developed using a very specific set of rules (process) and a unique language. While the scenarios themselves are clearly products of imagination and have no value in and of themselves, they help participants create knowledge that they can use in decision making. They also allow everyone involved to develop insights that will help them see subtle changes they might not otherwise have seen.

Budgeting

Finally, there is budgeting, which is likely not an activity that most people associate with play. However, when we take a closer look, we notice that the activities involved in the ideal budgeting process clearly exhibit some of the qualities that define play with a purpose, and are linked very closely to the three defining characteristics of serious play. The clearly and explicitly defined purpose is to imagine what can be produced and sold, and where it can be produced and sold, not actually to produce, buy, or sell anything. In budgeting, participants typically imagine what the organization is going to produce or deliver in a given time frame, and what kind of investments it would require. So, it follows the first and second characteristics of serious play. Finally, the participants in the budgeting process follow the very specific language of numbers and accounting, and rules about how things add up and for which period this is relevant. This is not a language or set of rules that most managers use in other contexts, which makes it fit with the third characteristic of serious play.

Of course, budgeting does not always follow the steps of serious play. It's often corrupted to represent something very different (e.g., competing for resources or setting oneself up to succeed). However, budgeting in its purest form can be categorized as serious play.

RESOURCES

Below we mention a number of books as well as a website that describe processes that demonstrate serious play characteristics:

- The army and war games: Pax Ludens, www.paxludens.org/
- Strategy making: *Playing to Win* by A. G. Lafley and Roger L. Martin (Harvard Business School Publishing, 2013); *Good Strategy/Bad Strategy* by Richard Rumelt

(Crown Business, 2011); *Must-Win Battles* by Peter Killing and Thomas Malknight with Tracey Keys (Prentice Hall, 2006)

- Scenario planning/development: *The Sixth Sense* by Kees van der Heijden et al. (John Wiley & Sons, 2002), *Scenarios* by Kees van der Heijden (John Wiley & Sons, 2nd ed., 2005), and *Transformative Scenario Planning* by Adam Kahane (Berrett-Koehler, 2012)

The need, the LEGO brick, and the concept of serious play are all essential elements in what comes together as the LEGO SERIOUS PLAY method. We will now turn to what it is that defines the method.

CHAPTER 4

The LEGO® SERIOUS PLAY® Method

The LEGO SERIOUS PLAY method is a regular and systematic way of accomplishing what we have described in previous chapters using the LEGO brick and the serious play concepts as the dominant levers.

As noted earlier, the need that sparked the initial idea for LEGO SERIOUS PLAY did *not* come from a desire to develop a method that helps groups and individuals think, communicate, and solve problems together—not by any stretch of the imagination. Rather, the impetus was exclusively to use the combination of bricks and playing seriously to *help an executive team bring more imagination* into their strategy development. Today, we refer to the solution to this particular challenge as the LEGO SERIOUS PLAY Real Time Strategy For the Enterprise application. This is a particular strategy workshop in which the method is applied.

When we look at the LEGO SERIOUS PLAY method, we typically split the definition into three parts:

1. It is a systematic set of group dynamic principles.
2. It is a set of principles for the systematic use of the LEGO brick.
3. It is the systematic use of the LEGO SERIOUS PLAY techniques, which consist of a Core Process and seven Application Techniques (ATs).

The three parts are intertwined and inseparable. Try to use only one of them without the others and it simply won't work—and couldn't be categorized as LEGO SERIOUS PLAY.

The purpose of the group dynamic procedures is to destroy the 20/80 meeting syndrome, a trend we first discussed in Chapter 1. This is a situation where 20 percent of the participants in the meeting use 80 percent of the time to talk about *their* knowledge and *their* intentions. The goal with LEGO SERIOUS PLAY is instead to create what we refer to as a 100/100 meeting—one where everyone present feels compelled to bring their insights to the table, and can maximize their confidence and commitment to their fullest potential.

We can summarize the principles for the group dynamic procedures as follows:

- Requiring everyone to participate *all the time* (100/100)
- Requiring everyone to participate in *all the phases* of the LEGO SERIOUS PLAY process

- Introducing the LEGO SERIOUS PLAY process in a form that is *inclusive for all*
- Leading the group as a *facilitator*, not a consultant, trainer, teacher, or instructor
- Facilitating a 100 percent *democratic process*
- Giving people *time to reflect and gather their thoughts* before anyone begins to talk

The purpose of the systematic use of the LEGO brick is to make the models—not any individual present—the center of attention in the meeting. The principles for the systematic use of the LEGO brick are:

- The LEGO brick is used to *unlock and construct new knowledge*, not to convey someone's answer or knowledge.
- There is *no one right way* to build with the LEGO bricks.
- Everyone has an *obligation to build* and the *right to tell the story* in the LEGO model.
- The *builder owns* the LEGO model and its story.
- You *must accept the builder's meaning* and story in the LEGO model.
- *Question the LEGO model* and its story—not the person.

The LEGO SERIOUS PLAY techniques include a four-step Core Process (see Figure 4.1) and a set of seven clearly defined Application Techniques (Figure 4.2) that are described in the following sections.

Let's take a look at each model in detail.

THE CORE PROCESS

The Core Process is the basic operating system in the LEGO SERIOUS PLAY method. It is the syntax in a language that helps the participants put into words what they know and don't know they know. The questions which are posed in step 1 of the Core Process will determine the content of steps 2, 3, and 4.

The Core LEGO SERIOUS PLAY Process
Step 1 Posing the Question
Step 2 Construction
Step 3 Sharing
Step 4 Reflection

FIGURE 4.1   The Core LEGO SERIOUS PLAY Process
© 2014 Association of Master Trainers.

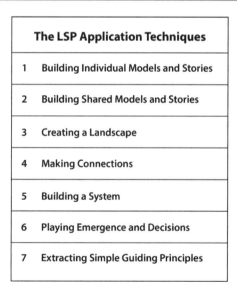

The LSP Application Techniques	
1	Building Individual Models and Stories
2	Building Shared Models and Stories
3	Creating a Landscape
4	Making Connections
5	Building a System
6	Playing Emergence and Decisions
7	Extracting Simple Guiding Principles

FIGURE 4.2   The LEGO SERIOUS PLAY Application Techniques
© 2014 Association of Master Trainers.

Step 2, constructing, is the building and thinking time during which the participants build LEGO models and stories which answer the question that was asked. It is important to note that when building something concrete the participants are also building new insights and connections in their minds (see Chapter 6). Step 3, sharing, naturally follows step 2. Everyone now gets to share their story and model; this version of distributed dialogue ensures that everyone's perspective and insight is shared. The Core Process is completed with step 4, reflecting, where after each story the facilitator and the other participants reflect on what they have heard, and maybe on what they can see in the model but do not understand. Reflecting takes the form of asking questions about what can be seen in the model, what different elements mean.

It's important to note that there are no standard questions in the LEGO SERIOUS PLAY method. The questions the facilitator asks will depend entirely on the issues the group is addressing. All questions are unique to the topics/challenges that people are exploring and dealing with through the use of the method. Both the Core Process and the seven Application Techniques are *processes without content*—until the facilitator adds content to achieve the desired objectives for the intervention with the LEGO SERIOUS PLAY method.

Combined with the group dynamic principles and LEGO brick principles described earlier, the Core Process's four steps ensure that the LEGO SERIOUS PLAY method always delivers on these objectives:

- Get *100 percent participation* from everyone in the group.
- Give *all participants time to think* before they speak.
- Hear and be able to *appreciate every person's unique insight* on the issue being discussed.
- Get all participants to *step up to the plate* and be part of the discussion and decision making.
- *Communicate* in a way that:
  - Helps everyone *express* his or her *thoughts* and insights.

- Helps the listener *understand* and *remember* what people say.
- *Minimizes* the risks of *misunderstandings* and miscommunications.
- Provides *equal* support for a variety of communication styles (auditory, visual, and kinesthetic).
- Helps all participants *focus on the message*, not the messenger.

We experienced a breakthrough moment in the development of the LEGO SERIOUS PLAY method when we recognized the importance of the following four factors. Indeed, we've found that they are highly critical for achieving success with the process for the full duration of the workshop, particularly when people experience the method for the first time.

Factor 1: Each participant must start with a set of bricks identical with everyone else's sets.

Factor 2: Each participant must begin by constructing his or her own LEGO model and story.

Factor 3: The participants come to see the brick as a metaphor and not as a metonym. A metaphor is a figure of speech that describes the topic by asserting that it is on some level similar to the object used—for example, the LEGO model—even though they are otherwise very different (e.g., the competition is like a fox, cunning and fast). As mentioned in Chapter 1, a metonym is also a figure of speech, but there the object simply stands in for (represents) the object.

Factor 4: A 100 percent safe, highly structured, and foolproof hands-on introduction to the Core Process is necessary within the first 45 to 60 minutes of the workshop.

Despite the fact that each LEGO SERIOUS PLAY workshop is unique—that is, it's designed to meet the specific objectives of the intervention—the workshop's introduction always follows the same structure, syntax, and progression to accommodate these four critical factors.

THE SEVEN APPLICATION TECHNIQUES

Each of the seven Application Techniques (see Figure 4.2) has a specific purpose and function in the LEGO SERIOUS PLAY method, depending on the objectives of the LEGO SERIOUS PLAY workshop.

Here is a short description of each of the seven Application Techniques (ATs).

AT 1: Building Individual Models and Stories

The purpose of AT 1 is for each individual to unlock new knowledge, and subsequently be able to communicate this knowledge to the other people in the group. The goal here is to share the knowledge that's currently only living in his or her mind and get it onto the table where everyone can see it.

The example to the left in Figure 4.3 represents someone's knowledge of trust, whereas the example to the right represents someone's unlocked knowledge about a

FIGURE 4.3   AT 1 in Use: Building Individual Models and Stories to Unlock New Knowledge

company's identity, where the core is creative, dynamic, and disorganized and driven by four people of whom two are more dominant. The frame represents an external view of the company as very colorful and very structured.

AT 2: Building Shared Models and Stories

The purpose of AT 2 is for the team to make decisions about shared understanding of a given topic by consolidating a number of individual models of this topic into one shared model. The use of AT 2 is always preceded by the use of AT 1. The example to the left in Figure 4.4 shows the process in play, and the example to the right shows how the group has constructed their shared model (the model in the middle of the table) using components from their individual models (AT 1) unlocking their knowledge about the topic being explored.

AT 3: Creating a Landscape

The purpose of AT 3 is analyzing, categorizing, and seeing similarities, differences, patterns, and so on among a collection of individual models without losing any original

FIGURE 4.4   AT 2 in Use: Building Shared Models and Stories to Reach a Shared Decision

FIGURE 4.5   AT 3 in Use: Creating a Landscape to Analyze the Variables and See the Bigger Picture

details or meanings. The examples in Figure 4.5 show two uses of this technique to chunk knowledge.

AT 4: Making Connections

The aim here is to identify relationships between the meanings of two previously constructed LEGO models by building a physical link between two or more previously constructed LEGO models (see Figure 4.6). When making connections, the LEGO building material can also be part of the story itself (e.g., the difference between using a chain, string, or tube for the connection).

AT 5: Building a System

Here, participants explore and identify systems and their impact. In this way, AT 5 is an extension of AT 4, making connections. When multiple models are connected in such a way that a ripple effect or unforeseen impact might occur, we refer to it as a system. Building a system is a continuation of connections to build the entire web of connections as in Figure 4.7.

FIGURE 4.6 AT 4 in Use: Making Connections to Identify the Relationships and Their Characteristics between the Variables

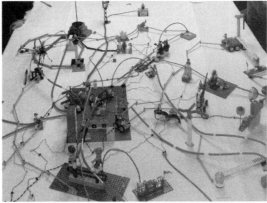

FIGURE 4.7 AT 5 in Use: Building a System to Map the Complex Web Connecting the Variables

AT 6: Playing Emergence and Decisions

The aim of AT 6 is to *strategize*—that is, play out scenarios and decisions to explore and probe how the system is impacted by and will respond to multiple unpredictable dynamic events and different choices of strategy. AT 5 is a prerequisite for a rich and full AT 6. In the illustration in Figure 4.8 the group is playing emergence and testing decisions with the previously developed system.

AT 7: Extracting Simple Guiding Principles

Finally, the goal of AT 7 is to develop something we refer to as Simple Guiding Principles. These are developed through the learning and information gleaned from

FIGURE 4.8   AT 6 in Use: Playing Emergence and Testing Decisions to Gain Insights about How the Systems React to Changes and Explore the Impact of Decisions Taken in Response to These Changes in the System

the previous steps, in particular AT 6. The function of Simple Guiding Principles is to support strategic decision making in real time. They emerge as a result of playing with the system in the previous Application Technique.

Something that's essential to note is that one doesn't need to employ the seven Application Techniques in order; that is, it's *not a linear process* from AT 1 to AT 7. It always begins with AT 1, but from there it can go on to AT 2, or jump to AT 3 or AT 4 as an example.

However, in cases such as AT 6 and AT 7, AT 1 to AT 5 are necessary intermediary steps for the full experience.

In general, while the complexity of the Application Technique increases as you move up or down the scale, so does the value you create in each step.

THE FACILITATOR TRAPS

LEGO SERIOUS PLAY is a facilitated method; it takes someone to guide the progression, to keep the play serious and risk free, and to ensure progression. Building and telling stories with the LEGO bricks will almost always be fun and enjoyable. However, a trained and skilled facilitator is invaluable to achieve specific business, team, or personal development objectives. Facilitators undergo comprehensive training before they engage in designing and facilitating with end users.

The facilitator's responsibilities are to lead the process while respecting the principles for the group dynamics listed above, the use of the LEGO bricks, and the use of the Core Process and Application Techniques. The facilitators must do this in accordance with the specifications provided to them during their training. The facilitator's role is not to convey an answer or specific knowledge about the complex issue that the workshop participants are trying to deal with. They are simply there to help the participants find the solution within their own system. The facilitators are trained to do this by framing and asking the relevant questions using the Core Process and appropriate Application Techniques.

We have seen many outstanding facilitators during our 12 years with LEGO SERIOUS PLAY; we've also witnessed a few who were less than outstanding. As a result, we began to compile a list of what we call "facilitator traps" several years ago. We've seen the following top five traps emerge over the years.

Trap 1: The Facilitator Becomes a Consultant

It's clear that the facilitator has fallen into this trap when he or she starts drawing the conclusions, giving advice, and taking charge of the meeting. The impact you experience is a group almost immediately falling out of flow.

Trap 2: The Facilitator Forgets What It Is Like When Participants Are Not Yet Familiar with the Process

The LEGO SERIOUS PLAY method is still a highly unusual, counterintuitive, and boundary-breaking experience for most people in the business world. That requires the facilitator to be very careful with the framing and goal setting so it does not become all about the LEGO bricks. Another way of falling into this trap is when the facilitator does not use the so-called skills building (see Chapter 8) in the beginning of the workshop to help the participants familiarize themselves with the method, the bricks, and the use of metaphors.

Trap 3: The Facilitator Comes to the Rescue Too Soon

The LEGO SERIOUS PLAY method is designed to push people out of their comfort zones. Occasionally, participants become (or start out!) frustrated; they're looking for someone to step in and give directions and answers to the challenges they are encountering. It is during these times of frustration that the most powerful learning is happening—so as much as a facilitator might want to, coming to the rescue too soon by taking control and responsibility for finding answers is seldom a good idea.

This could, for example, happen during AT 3 when the participants are creating a landscape out of individual models. At this point the participants often struggle, trying to find an overarching narrative that ties the models together; thus it is tempting for the facilitator to come to the rescue with an observation that would make the placing seem easier.

While it's an easy trap to fall into, it's one that the facilitator should make an effort to avoid, as should leaders in most cases, but that is a different story. What typically happens if a facilitator falls into the trap is that it feels easier for the participants, but less insight is created and the participants are less committed to the result.

Trap 4: The Facilitator Lets the Story Run Away from the LEGO Model

This happens when a facilitator allows participants to go off on tangents about topics *not* represented in their LEGO construction. Typically, the participant either does a long preamble to the story or continues talking after having shared the story in the model. When continuing, you usually see such participants sit up straighter, then lean back and start looking nowhere in particular; this is when they switch into the standard arguments and pet projects. Very soon the rest of the group will adopt a similar posture; they will lean out, and their attention will be lost. The participants are interested in the new insight; they want to hear the story about the model, not stories about everything else, and the facilitator needs to make this the focus of the workshop.

Trap 5: The Facilitator Does Not Have a Plan B

As previously discussed, the LEGO SERIOUS PLAY method is a democratic and participant-driven approach to dealing with complex issues that are real and relevant to everyone in the intervention workshop. It therefore empowers people when they're able to think, communicate, and express themselves. However, when you put such forces into motion, the result can be different from your predictions. One can never predict exactly what will come out in a building round, whether individual or shared; surprising new insights may emerge, or perhaps the shared model building reveals that there are two very different understandings of the same thing. In other cases the stories from one round make it clear that instead of talking about customers, for example, what is needed is to explore the organizational competencies.

Thus, the LEGO SERIOUS PLAY method not only requires a well-thought-out process flow, but it also requires the facilitator to heed the need for modifications or alterations in the blink of an eye. The facilitator needs as a minimum to know which parts to skip if one part takes longer than expected, or, even better, he or she should have a full plan B ready. A full plan B would be in the form of an alternative road map design, so if X happens, then this is what we will do. The facilitator must also be ready to develop a plan C at the blink of an eye should the workshop turn in an unpredictable direction.

APPLYING THE LEGO SERIOUS PLAY METHOD

The complex challenges where leaders and teams look to the LEGO SERIOUS PLAY method for help typically fall within one of three domains depicted in Figure 4.9.

Enterprise development covers a wide range of areas within strategy, business, organizational, innovation, and product development, as well as learning and education. In short, it includes any complex issue that is not focused on either team or personal development. The overlapping of the ovals indicates that there is always some level of both team and personal development taking place whenever you apply the LEGO SERIOUS PLAY method for a group.

We deliberately use the term *development* in all three areas. Earlier in this section we described the three core needs we are addressing with the LEGO SERIOUS PLAY method, shown again in Figure 4.10.

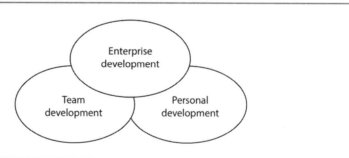

FIGURE 4.9   Enterprise, Team, or Personal Development

FIGURE 4.10   The Essential Purpose of the LEGO SERIOUS PLAY Method

The common denominator for all three needs is the desire to use our imaginations to first visualize and then reach a state that is different from the current state. That might involve developing a new strategy, a better business model, a set of new cultural values, a new vision, a more effective team, or a more innovative culture. We refer to this journey as getting from A, the current state, to B, the new state.

We mentioned earlier that the LEGO SERIOUS PLAY method is for courageous leaders in organizations and groups that are facing a complex challenge. One way of defining *complexity* in this instance is that it involves multiple stakeholders operating in a dynamic environment with a certain level of unpredictability. It is a situation that makes it impossible to move from A to B in a straight line, as shown in Figure 4.11 by path 1 from A to B. For example, when a department wants to work from the current

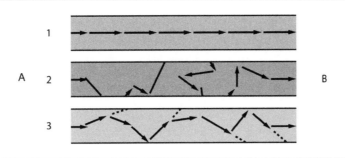

FIGURE 4.11   Three Possible Ways of Getting from Your Starting Point to Your Goal

value proposition to a new one, a number of stakeholders and their various wishes and agendas may impact the path.

Some of the courageous leaders who opt to utilize the LEGO SERIOUS PLAY method have experienced the difficulty of trying to move in a linear sequence (path 1). Attempting to solve an issue based on the assumption that they can make a detailed plan for getting from A to B can introduce obstacles. Often, it results in never getting to B at all (path 2); this could be because the system responds completely differently from what was expected and in a nonlinear way, and this was never tested. Or perhaps a particular stakeholder had not been heeded.

In contrast, we see how the LEGO SERIOUS PLAY method deals with complex issues in path 3. Leaders who undertake this method accept that getting from A to B will be a zigzagging process—one that can be successful only if you are able to get everyone involved, unlock tacit and new knowledge, and break habitual thinking.

Later in the book we will walk you through a number of actual case examples where LEGO SERIOUS PLAY has been applied to enterprise, team, or personal development. But before we do that, we will contemplate the LEGO SERIOUS PLAY etiquette and then step back and take you through some of the scientific theories that underpin the methodology.

CHAPTER 5

Contemplating the LEGO® SERIOUS PLAY® Territory

THE LEGO SERIOUS PLAY ETIQUETTE

The dictionary defines etiquette as: "the forms and practices prescribed by social convention or by authority." The LEGO SERIOUS PLAY etiquette it is a little different. The etiquette summarizes the experiences, science, forms, and practices that have evolved over time.

The etiquette falls into three major parts:

1. *Beliefs* or underlying values for engaging in a LEGO SERIOUS PLAY process
2. *Process* or how you as a facilitator act, i.e., your behavior.
3. *Group dynamics* or how the group acts and behaves—the behavior that you facilitate into existence

The topics that follow might seem to deal with subtle nuances of behavior, but they are merely maintaining the natural relationships of human beings involved in sustained serious play. The topics start with beliefs, continue with process, and then move into group dynamics.

Who Is Responsible for Adhering to the LEGO SERIOUS PLAY Etiquette?

The LEGO SERIOUS PLAY method is for groups and teams. Any process has either a certified facilitator or a process leader, who enables the process in accordance with the process laid out in the etiquette.

When your role is *facilitator*, you are not part of the process itself for the group. You can assist with building, but only on a technical level—how to get the bricks to stick together the way the participants want. You don't build your own models or tell your own stories.

When your role is *process leader* for a group that is already familiar with the method, you are part of the process for the group. You then participate in the process on the same level as everyone else. You construct, give meaning, and make stories like the others in the group.

Being a process leader is a very different role than that of the facilitator; as a process leader you are a member of the system in which the answer is anchored, whereas as a facilitator you help that system uncover its own answer, without assuming that you have it (being a nonmember of that system).

Beliefs

The answer is in the system.

The complex issue has emerged in the system, and in the same system the answer can be found. The LEGO SERIOUS PLAY process helps the members of the system to move to a new knowledge level where that answer is constructed (i.e., to expand the system).

Anyone can use the LEGO SERIOUS PLAY method.

The only requirement is hands (or feet). LEGO building experts have no advantage at all. You always have a chance to learn the techniques and the skill set before you are challenged with the complex issue. We never identify anyone in front of others as an expert in LEGO SERIOUS PLAY.

It is not about modeling.

LEGO SERIOUS PLAY is about unlocking knowledge and constructing new knowledge; it is not about making a physical representation of what something looks like. It is about the story you are able to tell using your model.

It is not about conveying someone's answer or knowledge.

The LEGO SERIOUS PLAY method is not about making people agree with decisions already made; it is about creating knowledge to solve problems. It is about surfacing and clarifying insights.

Process

Workshops with the LEGO SERIOUS PLAY method are always about using the bricks to construct and share the story, and the process always moves from individual to shared: the real power of the process is in this sequence.

If you skip the construction and just talk, the effectiveness of the whole approach is lost. By skipping the construction of a model and thus of new knowledge, participants typically fall back on reproducing existing socially acceptable truths. If you construct and don't talk, new meaning will be created individually, but remain tacit; it will never emerge or be shared.

LEGO SERIOUS PLAY challenges always start with individual models. This ensures the sharing of original new knowledge and keeps all participants in the flow.

LEGO SERIOUS PLAY Always Requires at Least Two People

It is a process for meetings. When there are only two people and one is the process leader, *both* take equal part in the process of constructing, giving meaning, and making the story.

Always Frame the Challenge So It Is Clear

Make sure participants understand why they are building and making stories about this topic or issue, and that they will be making a story using the model. At the same time, the framing should be sufficiently open for each participant to construct her or his own knowledge and meaning about the given issue.

Provide them with instructions about how much time they have (short, medium, or long time), and also any other criteria that they have to take into consideration before they start building.

Trust the Process, and Return to the Model

If passions run high, leading to disagreements or misunderstandings, *do not* try to get protagonists to discuss a difference or talk it over face-to-face. Refocus questions and explanations to aim them firmly at the models, and away from the people. It works!

Group Dynamics

The goal in LEGO SERIOUS PLAY is to create what we refer to as a 100/100 meeting—one where everyone present feels compelled to bring their insights to the table, and can maximize their confidence and commitment to their fullest potential. Here is more a detailed description of how the LEGO SERIOUS PLAY etiquette ensures that.

Everyone Participates in Every Phase

There is no such thing as saying: "I can't think of anything to build" or "I don't have a story to tell" or "You can skip me this time."

If this happens, it means one individual is trying to unhook from the process. Like having one player sitting down in the middle of the basketball court, it could fragment the flow for others. This flow is established very naturally in the beginning of the process. Allowing one participant all of the sudden to become an observer, and thus not allow himself or herself to be vulnerable, also means that the remaining participants would indeed become vulnerable. It would introduce a power game into the workshop.

When You Don't Know What to Build, Start Building Anyway

Research has shown that using the hand initiates ideas that will not come by thinking alone. So if builders are stuck, encourage them to start building—anything. It always works. Don't have a planning meeting with yourself about what to build.

There Is No One Right Way to Build

You will never be given building instructions (a blueprint) for what to build and how to build. It is not about modeling someone else's story—it is about giving form to your inner thoughts and ideas.

If you can't build it with the bricks, *build it with your words*. Sometimes the urgency of the idea will outpace your ability to deliver the full construction of metaphors in time! So carry on with passion and expressive hands and use words to give meaning to what is in the model; as we say below, sometimes any brick can be given a particular meaning.

It's Your Meaning in the Model

The bricks don't have any particular inherent meaning in them, or any predecided iconic value—not even people or barrels or wheels. Whatever the builder says something represents that is what it is! Ask the builder to clarify the meaning, but never criticize the builder's choice of metaphor.

When I Am Asked to Build, You Must Listen to My Story

In other words, every individual who has built something must also have the opportunity to then make the story with the model and to share its meaning with others. Building a model and then not being able to share its story is completely meaningless to others and destructive and demoralizing for the builder.

When I Am Asked to Tell My Story, You Must Accept It, Too

Not only must every story be heard, but you must also accept what people bring up. It may not always be what you want to hear, and you may not even agree but be assured it will still be a valuable insight offered by the least threatening and most constructive method possible.

Question the Model and Its Story, Not the Person

Always ask questions to get more and clearer meaning—for the builder as well as the listener. But always ask about the model and the relationship between the model and the story, not the person and his or her intentions and reasons. Questioning the person's motives can destroy confidence and fragment the group. By making the questions about the model, we take the conflict out and the dialogue is moved from a personal relationship level to the object. Questions mean creating new knowledge, as we make new connections in our brains by giving new meaning to the model.

The Builder Owns the Model

Whatever you build is yours and is sacred. Others cannot edit or even move any part of it unless they ask permission and you agree with the way they are remaking the story. Neither can you ever take someone's model apart without getting permission first from the builder.

Stay in the Flow

Even as insights and issues are transferred to paper for later discussions, there still may be a strong temptation to instantly break off to discuss implications. As a general rule, don't go off at a tangent to the process unless it's clearly decided to do so.

It Must Be Hard Fun to Be Memorable

You will be challenged to the edge of your capabilities in a workshop based on the LEGO SERIOUS PLAY method, but never beyond. It is supposed to be hard fun, which will make it exhilarating and sometimes exhausting.

In Part I we focused on the territory of LEGO SERIOUS PLAY, the key concepts. In Part II we turn to the theories that have helped form and further the development of the method.

PART

LEGO® SERIOUS PLAY®: The Science Platform

Part II of the book will present the scientific domains within the learning, psychology, and neighboring fields from which the LEGO SERIOUS PLAY method grew, and in which we have found the insights that helped evolve the method and the understanding of how it creates results.

These results come from the participants' learning. In this book we several times talk about learning. In short, to us, learning simply means making sense of an experience and incorporating that experience into our own mental models of the world. This making sense is a fully creative activity. We must do it for ourselves; no one else can do it for us.

For example, when reading about flow in Chapter 8, you will go through such a learning experience and connect any new knowledge with what you already know and can relate to. We do not know what you already know and cannot make the connections for you. You are the sole builder of these connections.

However, before we dive further into the theories, it is important to stress that the LEGO SERIOUS PLAY method is not based on any new or groundbreaking science. Rather, as mentioned previously, it is the result of action research and evidence drawn from a variety of disciplines and proven research. Some of this was already firmly anchored inside the LEGO Company, and some emerged during the development and the implementation of LEGO SERIOUS PLAY. It is these disciplines that we will present in the following chapters. We'll then outline how we apply and see each in LEGO SERIOUS PLAY, and how this adds value for the participants.

In order to bring the application of (some of) the theories to life, we have included a small number of hands-on exercises. Thus, it will be helpful to have a couple of LEGO bricks within reach when you are reading this part. We suggest you go and find them now.

CHAPTER 6
Building Knowledge—Giving Your Mind a Hand

Without the LEGO bricks, there would be no LEGO® SERIOUS PLAY® method. The bricks are to the process like sunlight is to a solar cell; without sunlight, no energy is produced. Yet many people who have not experienced LEGO SERIOUS PLAY find the process puzzling. They wonder why building and telling stories with LEGO bricks is a more effective use of the team's time than employing traditional methods for dealing with and finding solutions to complex problems and challenges—like merely talking.

It can also be a challenge to both understand and accept that *children's* preferred way to learning about the world—through concrete hands-on interaction—is indeed also a more efficient method for adults. Many find it inconceivable that such a learning process works more effectively than using formal abstract thinking and communication in the form for words, tables, spreadsheets, and graphs.

This chapter presents you with the theories that address three topics intimately connected to the use of the LEGO bricks:

1. Building knowledge by building things in the world
2. Concrete thinking versus formal abstract thinking
3. Using the hand as the leading edge of the mind

Let's look at each in detail.

BUILDING KNOWLEDGE BY BUILDING THINGS IN THE WORLD

In short, we build knowledge by building things!

Try this: think about the aspects of your work that are especially motivating for you—the activities and events and people that give you energy and *really* engage you. While you think about this, take a pile of LEGO bricks to build a small LEGO model that expresses one of these aspects in a visual way. This undertaking will enable you to explain to a nine-year-old what you find highly motivating and energizing in your work. (See Figure 6.1.)

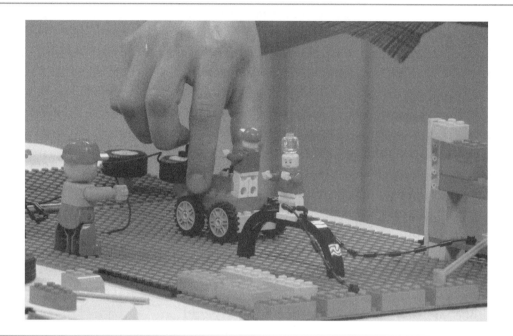

FIGURE 6.1   Don't Have a Meeting with Yourself About What to Build. Just Start Building and Let Your Hands Take Charge

Do not worry about making a plan before you start building. Just start putting some bricks together in a more or less structured way while simultaneously considering what it is you want the nine-year-old to understand. You have four to five minutes. Let your hands take over the control.

Now you have completed the two first steps in the LEGO SERIOUS PLAY Core Process. We have asked you a question (step 1) and you have built a LEGO model with meaning (step 2). It is time to move on to step 3—sharing the story. You can do this in one of two ways: (1) with someone else—a nine-year-old (as we suggested in the example), your spouse, or your colleague—or (2) with yourself. If you choose yourself, write down the main points of your story, or you may even opt to record it on your smartphone for review and perhaps to share it later on.

Let us move on to step 4 in the LEGO SERIOUS PLAY Core Process: learning and reflecting. This is your opportunity to provide the following information:

My work is _____.
And what I like the most is _____.
The reason that part is motivating is _____.

What you have experienced with this hands-on task is constructivism and constructionism at work. The building process helped and forced you to gather your thoughts about the topic. Some thoughts were likely very clear for you from the very beginning, while others were more vague and emerged during the building and/or the sharing process. But the process as a whole enabled you to pull together your sum of insights and communicate this to both yourself and others. You have *built knowledge by building things.*

Constructivism

Let us step back and look at renowned developmental psychologist Jean Piaget's theory of constructivism to explain what is happening when we "build knowledge by building things."

Jean Piaget is the father of constructivism, perhaps best known for his stage theory of child development. But even more fundamental than this was his theory that children don't simply acquire knowledge bit by bit. Rather, they use their experience in the world to construct coherent, robust frameworks called "knowledge structures." They aren't just passive absorbers of experience and information, but active theory builders.

In one of his more famous experiments, Piaget discovered that young children believe that water can change in amount when poured from a short, wide glass into a tall, thin one. These children have built a theory—which indeed, works most of the time—that states "taller means more." They undoubtedly created this theory through many experiences (measuring children's heights back-to-back, building block towers, amount of milk in one glass) and developed it into a robust structure. Mere insistence could not convince these children that the amount of water did not change. In other words, you could not simply tell these children the right answer; they wouldn't believe you if you did. They would have to build a new, more sophisticated knowledge structure, taking into account the theory, again based on their experience, that "wider can also mean more." This would help them consider that the amount of water does not change when it is poured from one glass to the other.

Thus, constructivism states that children—and really, anyone learning something for the first time—are not simply empty vessels into whom we can pour knowledge. Rather, they are theory builders who construct and rearrange that knowledge based on what they already know and have experienced.

Constructionism

Now let us turn our attention to Seymour Papert, a colleague of Piaget in the late 1950s and early 1960s. Though he agreed with Piaget's theory of constructivism, he wanted to extend the premise to the fields of learning theory and education.

Papert sought to create a learning environment that was more conducive to Piaget's theories. He saw conventional school environments as too sterile, too passive, too dominated by instruction; they didn't provide or promote an atmosphere that allowed children to be the active builders that he knew they were.

Papert eventually called his theory "constructionism." It included everything associated with Piaget's constructivism, but went a step beyond. If we believe that we hold knowledge as structures based on our interaction with the world, then we can *create knowledge* faster and better (learning) when we are engaged in constructing a product or something external to themselves—a sand castle, a machine, a computer program, or a book. In short, "When you build in the world, you build in your mind."

Since constructionism incorporates and builds upon Piaget's theory of constructivism, two types of construction are actually going on, each reinforcing the other. When people construct things out in the world, they simultaneously assemble theories and knowledge structures in their minds. This new knowledge then enables them to build even more sophisticated things out in the world, which yields still more knowledge, and so on, in a self-reinforcing cycle. This supports a central tenet of the LEGO SERIOUS PLAY method: learning happens especially well when we actively construct something physical/concrete that is external to us.

Papert first began thinking about constructionism in the late 1960s, after observing a group of students become deeply and actively engaged in creating soap sculptures in an art class over several weeks. Several things about the experience struck him: the children's level of engagement, the elements of creativity and originality in the actual products, how well the students were interacting and collaborating with one another, the longevity of the enterprise, and the sheer sense of fun and enjoyment that permeated the experience.

A mathematician by training, Papert could not help wondering why most mathematics classes were so unlike these art classes. Rather, he observed that math classes were dull, boring, unengaging, passive, and dominated by instruction—really, anything *but* fun. Why was this so? His own experience told him that mathematics could be exciting, beautiful, challenging, engaging, and every bit as creative as making soap sculptures. So why was something with so much potential being ruined for so many children?

Papert's contemplations about this observation led him on a many-year journey to design a more constructible approach to mathematics. He knew he would have to work with media more sophisticated and powerful than simple art materials. In the 1970s, Papert and his colleagues designed a computer programming language called Logo, which enabled children to learn mathematics by building pictures, animations, music, games, and simulations (among other things) on the computer.

Then, in the mid-1980s, members of his MIT (Massachusetts Institute of Technology) team developed LEGO TC Logo, which combined the computer language with the familiar LEGO brick. This new tool enabled children to control their LEGO structures by creating programs on the computer. The resulting behaviors of such machines can be arbitrarily complex. It was the repeated experience of watching children use these sorts of materials—not just in order to learn about mathematics and design, but to actually *be mathematicians and designers*—that led Papert to conclude: "Better learning will not come from finding better ways for the teacher to instruct, but from giving the learner *better opportunities to construct*."[1]

Thus, the essential learning driver in the LEGO SERIOUS PLAY method is the concept of constructionism: learning by building something you can identify with and be proud of, and about which you can think, "This is *my thing*." As Papert himself points out, "What we learn in the process of building things that we care about sinks much deeper into the subsoil of our mind than what anyone can tell us."[2]

Constructionism involves two types of construction: when you construct things out in the world, you simultaneously construct knowledge in your head. Instructionism, on the other hand, occurs when somebody tells you what that person thinks you ought to know, and sometimes instructionism is the better way. For example, children can learn about the meaning of traffic lights in two ways. You can tell them that green means go and red means stop or you can send them out in traffic and learn by experimenting. Telling people that the LEGO bricks can be used either as metonym or metaphor is also instructionism. Instructionism is not always the wrong thing to do; it's somewhat like a strong medicine. If it comes at the right time and at the right dosage, then it can indeed be helpful.

CONCRETE THINKING VERSUS FORMAL ABSTRACT THINKING

It's time for a little exercise to really bring this topic to life. In Figure 6.2, you'll see a picture of what in the LEGO language is called a 2 × 4 stud brick. This is the quintessential LEGO brick.

The two-dimensional illustration in Figure 6.3 shows three of these bricks stacked on top of each other. They are arranged in such a way that if we view the stack from one side the illustration looks like A, and looking at it from a second side it looks like B. But it is the same small model in both cases.

The task for you is to take a pen or pencil and—*without* using three real 2 × 4 bricks to help you—make a two-dimensional drawing of what this stack of three bricks looks like from a third side (not top and not bottom). Give yourself some time, because most likely you will find it quite challenging and maybe even impossible.

FIGURE 6.2   LEGO Brick

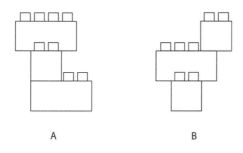

A   B

FIGURE 6.3   Two Views of the Same Stack of Three 2 × 4 Bricks

When you are done (or have given up), take three 2 × 4 bricks and stack them so they fit both the A and the B images—and maybe also your drawing. Do not feel discouraged if you did not get the drawing right the first time. Most of us are not able to do this without the help of the bricks unless we are trained in this kind of drawing technique. However, we should all be able to make the two-dimensional drawing if we can use (play with) the real 3-D bricks to assist our visualization. Thinking concretely with the bricks leads us much faster and more reliably to a formal abstract representation of the stack.

Let us look at another set of images that represent the same thing in three-dimensional and two-dimensional forms.

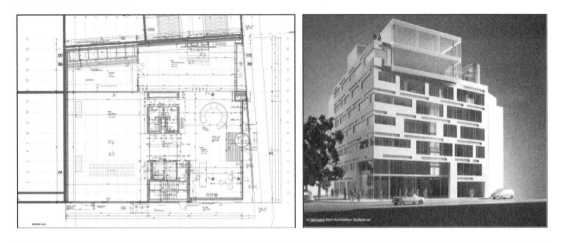

FIGURE 6.4   Making Two-Dimensional Representations of Things Is An Acquired Skill, Not Something that Is Natural for Us

The image of the building—shown to the right in Figure 6.4—represents a three-dimensional model and provides a number of advantages for both thinking and communication. It is much easier for your mind to imagine how it would be to live in the building and to play around with alternatives. The formal abstract representation shown in the blueprint at the left merely becomes the documentation of the thinking process.

With these two illustrations of the benefit of concrete thinking, let us return to Seymour Papert's work. Although his constructionism embraces and builds upon Piaget's constructivism, Papert eventually came to see some drawbacks to Piaget's stage theory—specifically, "his resistance to giving up the value system that places formal thinking 'on top.'" According to Papert, "This resistance led [Piaget] to see concrete thinking as children's thinking, and so keeps him from appreciating the full breadth of his discovery of the 'concrete' as a universal form of human reason."[3] In other words, Piaget saw abstract thinking as a higher level of thinking than concrete thinking. Concrete thinking for him was merely a stage you passed through. Once you had passed that stage, there would be no need to ever revert to the concrete mode of thinking.

Papert came to view the notion of concrete thinking/hands-on thinking not as a stage that children outgrow, but rather as a style of thinking that has its benefits and uses, just as logical or formal thinking has its benefits and uses. In other words, unlike Piaget, he didn't view concrete thinking as the cognitive equivalent of baby talk. Rather, he saw and explained it to others as a mode of thinking complementary to more abstract, formal modes of thought. In Papert's view, it is a grave mistake to forsake or cast off concrete thinking in favor of purely abstract thought. Doing so would seal oneself off from valuable modes of thinking and pathways to knowledge that isn't as accessible by other means.

USING THE HAND AS THE LEADING EDGE OF THE MIND

As we emphasized in Chapter 3, one of the needs that the LEGO SERIOUS PLAY method addresses is the unlocking of new knowledge. There is one angle that makes this challenge of unlocking knowledge even more daunting: *we don't know most of what we know*. In other words, we don't have a very thorough awareness of our own knowledge. The intricacies of our brains are partially to blame for this. As mentioned earlier, some of our knowledge is stored deeply in the brain, other elements are stored in different places in the cortex, or even the hippocampus. In other words, not everything is easily accessible.

The one comment from individuals that continues to stand out over our many years working with LEGO SERIOUS PLAY is: "I had no idea I knew this."

People sometimes articulate it more specifically like this:

I had no idea of how to begin to answer the question when you posed it, so I did what you have told us to do when we don't know what to build—I just started building. All of a sudden I realized that I had the answer in the LEGO model right in front of me.

We usually hear these comments when the participants have had to build an answer to a particularly complex question—one for which they really felt there was no (obvious) answer. Yet, to their surprise, they often succeed in finding one.

This ability of the LEGO SERIOUS PLAY method to draw out unconscious knowledge has proven to be considerably more powerful than we originally assumed. And it has led us to place a strong emphasis on these two words: *hand knowledge*. We use this to refer to what your hands know but your brain isn't entirely conscious of. For example, when you drive a car, your hands perform a range of tasks without your even having to realize it. However, there is one major difference in this comparison: when you drive a car, you *can* deliberately make yourself conscious about the knowledge your hands are applying by default. But you can become aware of the hand knowledge we refer to in LEGO SERIOUS PLAY only through the process of building with the hands *without* too much preplanning.

To help individuals use their hands as the leading edge of their mind and draw out the knowledge and insights, we offer them this ground rule: "Trust your hands." This is our way of encouraging them to let go and start building the answer to the question without having a plan for what to build and without knowing why they pick and put together the bricks they do. The "Trust your hands" ground rule is supplemented with a second ground rule: "Do not have a meeting with yourself about what to build; just start building."

We experience the power of these ground rules when people, after having solved a problem by building, will say something along the lines mentioned above: "I had no idea how to begin, but then I did what you told us—start building—and all of a sudden the solution emerged through my hands." This example is from a leadership development workshop in which the initial task was to unlock some of the participants' current insights about what is good leadership. The builder was stuck, yet all of a sudden the insight emerged as shown in Figure 6.5. The story is that good leadership is to know your leadership team's unique strengths and values and combine these in a way that brings together both the commonalities and the uniquenesses (i.e., the brick stack in the center).

FIGURE 6.5   One Way of Representing Good Leadership

In our journey with LEGO SERIOUS PLAY, we have not come across even one in-depth research that fully explains the concept of hand knowledge as we have experienced it. And we believe that the evolutionary aspect also comes into play.

Evolution

There is well-grounded scientific evidence that points to the profound interdependence of the hand and mind. The work of anthropologists and paleontologists like Louis and Mary Leakey, their son Richard Leakey, Donald Johanson, and Sherwood Washburn shows very clearly the development of this relationship.

Starting about 3.2 million years ago, the human ancestor species we call *Australopithecus afarensis* (the "Lucy" skeleton) was the first to show clear bipedalism—that is, walking on two legs only. This meant that the other extremities (specifically, the hands) were freed up to be used for other things. Already pentadactyl—that is, five-fingered—the hand of Lucy also begins to show the first clear signs of a modern opposable thumb. This is the crucial development that makes the human hand's precision motor grip possible. Lucy's brain size was about 400 to 500 cubic centimeters. The opposable thumb appears in a more clearly modern form with the species we call *Homo habilis*. This species is dated to about 2.1 million years ago, and has a brain size of 600 to 700 cubic centimeters.

Homo habilis is a watershed in the human experience, because it is the first prehuman species also associated with what are clearly manufactured tools—chipped stone implements used for pounding, cutting, cleaving, and so on. As Frank Wilson, author of the book *The Hand: How Its Use Shapes the Brain, Language and Human Culture*, explains, "the whole list of recently acquired and uniquely human behavioral attributes must have arisen during the long process of brain enlargement that began with the expansion of novel and inventive tool use by Homo habilis."[4]

The intimate link between the hand and the brain in human development appears clearly in modern human physiology. Canadian neurosurgeon Wilder Penfield (1891–1976) developed a map of the brain—depicted in Figure 6.6—that shows its proportions dedicated to controlling different parts of the body.

What immediately strikes one is the enormous size of the part devoted to the hand. While this clearly shows the profound interconnection between the hand and the brain, what does this have to do with the higher mental processes of abstraction and reasoning?

As one of the fathers of our modern understanding of intelligence, Jean Piaget introduced the idea that intelligence grows from the mind's interaction with the world. Thus, the complex, abstract ideas such as time, causality, and space are all active operations that grow from the feedback processes between the living mind and the encompassing world. A proselytizer of Piaget's work, Hans Furth, argues that the

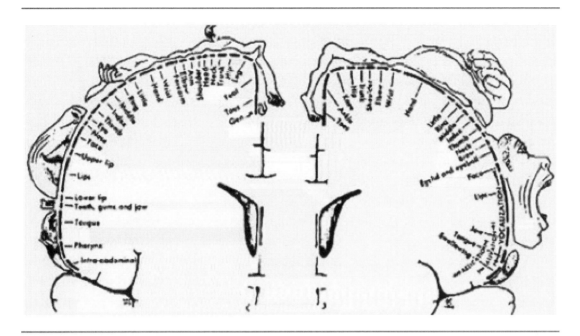

FIGURE 6.6   Penfield's Map of the Brain

Source: Reprinted from *The Cerebral Cortex of Man* by Wilder Penfield and Theodore Rasmussen, Macmillan Publishing, 1950.

key insight of the great psychologist's work is that "knowledge is an operation that constructs its objects."[5]

As we know from the work of human paleontologists, the connections between the hand and the mind are central to human development. This fact, together with Penfield's and Piaget's scientific insights, would suggest that using the hand to manipulate and construct the world is not only a profoundly *human* thing; it's also a primal way that the brain uses to construct its own knowledge of the world. We evolved to live in and master a three-dimensional world—and our brain mirrors this. Even as you read this, your brain is navigating the text by trying to understand the letters as physical objects; it simply does not know another way of understanding them.[6]

Contemplating Giving Your Mind a Hand

The LEGO SERIOUS PLAY method is inseparable from the theory of constructionism and the hands-on building process. It's not a simple visualizing modeling tool; it's a way of *thinking with objects* and through our hands to unleash creative energies, modes of thought, and ways of seeing that most adults have forgotten they even possessed. The method stakes its reputation on the belief that adults can dust off those modes of concrete thinking and put them to use again—and that when they do, great benefits are in store. One might even argue that you could use other kinds of concrete building materials, and that your materials don't necessarily have to be LEGO bricks. That is true; however, the variety, flexibility, reusability, modularity, and quick use of the building system makes the LEGO bricks superior to any other known concrete material.

A business or company is so much more than a building and the people in it. It is a vast network of connections and complicated relationships on many different levels. Conveying such abstract relationships on paper through graphs, flowcharts, block diagrams, and so on often fails to capture the dynamic nature of the enterprise. While computer modeling and simulations are a step up from static models, these too are limited. It is often very difficult to comprehend the totality of these complex relationships. The LEGO SERIOUS PLAY method is a bold approach that applies the power of constructionism to the complexity of the business world, thereby making the abstract network of interrelationships that make up any business concrete, appropriable, and comprehensible.

In our experience, when a LEGO SERIOUS PLAY representation of a business like the one shown in front to the right in Figure 6.7 is constructed—not of the buildings, but of the business in a systemic sense—people see things they can't see when they look at the business described in words and diagrams as shown to the left top in Fig. 6.7. The access to a three-dimensional metaphorical model of their business and its landscape allows them to visualize strategies that were formerly opaque and closed off to them. They can see their enterprise in a more holistic sense, and can manipulate it, play with it, and ask all sorts of what-if questions by physically altering it.

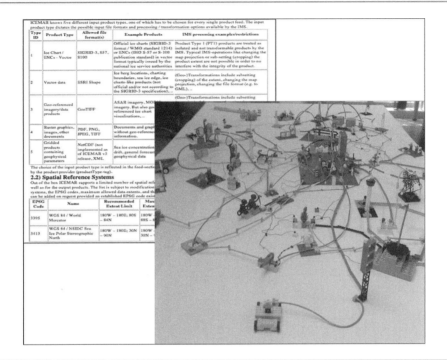

FIGURE 6.7 Two Different Ways to Represent a Business System

"What if our key supplier goes bankrupt?" "What if we relocated our marketing team to Asia?" "What if our sales suddenly doubled?"

As with the earlier example of the 3-D building where the ultimate goal is to produce a blueprint, the ultimate goal of the 3-D business might be to produce a written plan like that shown to the left in Figure 6.7. The LEGO SERIOUS PLAY method is a faster and more effective way of getting there through an engaging process that compels everyone to lean in and contribute 100 percent.

CHAPTER 7
Neuroscience—Understanding the Builder's Mind

Neuroscience is somewhat of a newcomer to the understanding of the LEGO® SERIOUS PLAY® method. In the early research phase, findings from neuroscience were used mostly on an intuitive level to support the method's development. However, as this branch of science has evolved, with the increasing use of functional magnetic resonance imaging (fMRI) and most recently functional near-infrared spectroscopy (fNIRS), many medical and research professionals are publishing papers that can help us understand and further strengthen the impact of LEGO SERIOUS PLAY.

Most neuroscientists would go to great lengths to stress that we're still in the early days of applying findings directly in workshops. This should of course be heeded—and it is with that in mind that we dive into the insights that *do* seem to be emerging from this exciting field. These are findings that support the reflections about constructionism, constructivism, and hand knowledge that we covered in Chapter 6, and we have clustered the insights into sections on attention, memory, and developing insights in this chapter.

ATTENTION

Emotions drive attention, which drives learning, which drives memory. We will return to emotions in the next chapter where we look at the flow theory and go into detail with the emotional aspect in relation to the LEGO SERIOUS PLAY method. However, first we turn our attention to attention.

We can define attention as the ability to focus on particular and relevant inputs, while inhibiting irrelevant information and stimuli. It is biologically impossible to learn and remember information that the brain has not paid attention to. Therefore, attention is essential in developing new solutions; but unfortunately, it is a scarce and easily depleted resource. To make matters worse, many of us have a tendency to use it counterproductively—that is, allowing it to be diverted to something immediately gratifying and/or not especially challenging. Similarly, when we belong to the 80 percent in the dreaded 20/80 meetings, we are often tempted to use it on things that are not relevant to our work—and therefore fail to remember information to which we haven't paid any attention.

Let's look closer at what characterizes attention.

Attention is a scarce resource: we can attend to only a limited number of things at once. When we try to attend to several things simultaneously, the quality of our work deteriorates and we form weaker memory links. Hence, there is really no such thing as multitasking. Focused attention increases the probability of engaging the hippocampus (we'll cover this more later) and consequently, an increased probability of successful memory formation.

The intensity of attention is often defined as *attention density*, which is specifically the number of observations paid to a particular idea per unit of time.[1] Thus, the more observations per unit of time or the more units of time, the higher attention density is. LEGO SERIOUS PLAY incorporates more types of observations per unit of time: we work with the auditory through the story, the visual through the model, and the kinesthetic through the physical touching.

Four elements help us keep our attention focused:

1. *Arousal*. We are *emotionally engaged* in whatever we do.
2. *Spatial orientation*. We need to *physically move around* and directly orient our bodies toward something; researchers specifically cite a three-step process of *disengaging*, *moving*, and *engaging*.
3. *Novelty detection and reward*. We sense something is *new* or can predict that there is some sort of *reward*.
4. *Executive organization*. We can see that the topic or purpose is *aligned with our goals*.

So how do we use the four elements to our advantage in the LEGO SERIOUS PLAY method?

Arousal: The participants become *emotionally engaged*—for example, by the use of powerful visual metaphors such as DUPLO animals (sharks, tigers, elephants, etc.). We will discuss these in more detail when we discuss the role of emotion in memory formation further in the following section.

Spatial orientation: Participants have to *disengage* from what they otherwise do as they get their hands on the LEGO bricks and engage in undisturbed building in response to the facilitator's questions. LEGO SERIOUS PLAY Application Techniques (see Chapter 4) such as shared model building and landscaping also activate spatial orientation. In this situation, participants disengage from a particular model or view of the model(s), move to a different position, and engage again. Finally, the room's setup that places special LEGO SERIOUS PLAY kits at a remote table to which the participants have to move may play an important role. Notice also how you disengaged from other activities (e.g., reading this book) when you built your model during Chapter 6. You probably physically put the book away or turned toward another part of the table.

Novelty detection and reward: Often, the very fact of building with LEGO bricks is in itself a novelty. In addition, the first time a participant uses LEGO SERIOUS PLAY, he or she will always start with his or her "own" kit. Participants will always get acknowledgment as a reward. We often observe this as participants find new answers to challenges and questions that have been with them or the organization for a long time. We also see this kind of reward as part of building stronger attention density.

Executive organization: Workshops always start with a clear framing of how the delivery ties in to the success of the participants' organization and/or their own goals. This makes it clear for the brain to attend to the process, and leads to a release of the neurotransmitter dopamine—something that helps shut out information that would be noise in this case.

The challenge that we all face—at work, in particular—is that the brain did not evolve to remain focused on the same stimuli for extended periods of time. If we try to do so, the brain yields diminishing returns over time. Its natural response is to interject its own down time. This is done in order to strengthen new synaptic connections related to what it has paid attention to. You may have experienced this yourself (e.g., needing to browse the Internet for moment or to go for a cup of coffee).

To help maintain the focus we ask people to turn off their mobile phones during workshops; we have them listen for understanding and look for patterns and deeper-lying questions. We also set up the room in such a way that they build their LEGO models in silence. Our goal in doing so is to have them create at a point where the individual units of each participant's brain come together in synchrony.

MEMORY FORMATION AND RETENTION

While we may talk about memory as if it is *one* thing, it is really several memory systems. The first distinction is between the long-term memory and the short-term or so-called working memory. The latter involves the in-the-moment handling of input—the stuff we hold present in our mind when we engage in work or dialogues. We use this memory, for example, when someone gives us a telephone number we have asked for and want to use right away to call, or when we are solving some sort of task or engaging in discussions.

We can break down long-term memory further into declarative and nondeclarative memory. Nondeclarative memory is the implicit memory; it includes things like physical skills, habits, and conditioned responses, and is believed to involve different parts of the brain than the declarative memory. Had this been a book about sports and had we worked as, for example, soccer coaches, then the focus might have been more on the nondeclarative memory.

The declarative memory can be further split into (1) the *episodic*, which is about events such as personal experiences from a particular time and place, and (2) the *semantic*, which focuses on facts, knowledge about the world, objects, and language. Understanding both aspects of the declarative memory is crucial in working with the LEGO SERIOUS PLAY method.

Both kinds are typically broken into three stages:

1. *Encoding and forming.* This is the formation of the actual memory in the brain.
2. *Retaining and retrieving.* This is keeping, accessing, and using the memory, such as in conversation.
3. *Encoding and strengthening.* This is reinforcing a memory that is already there. There is always the risk of losing a certain memory.

All of these stages are essential; one could say that learning includes easily retrieving memory of new knowledge. But first you need to *have something* to retrieve; hence, encoding/formation stands out as an obvious first key stage in creating results with LEGO SERIOUS PLAY.

Finally, before looking at how we can strengthen memory, there is one part of the brain that we must discuss: the hippocampus. This part of the brain is highly connected both with the relatively new part of the brain, the cortex, and to the older parts, the subcortical structures. It is at the core of memory formation and retrieval; some memory even seems to be stored there. You can think of it as your personal Google search and save engine that both helps to decide where to store and encode memory and also helps you retrieve it later.

So how can LEGO SERIOUS PLAY help participants improve memory? In addition to attention that we have already mentioned, scientists point to:

- Levels of processing
- The importance of context
- Generation
- Emotions

Levels of Processing

The more deeply we process information, the stronger memory formation is. We do not store information in one finished file like on a computer, but more as a web across the brain. Therefore, the more diverse and rich associations we have to a memory, the stronger the web. If the learner can also transform information into something personally meaningful, then that person will form an even stronger memory.

The LEGO SERIOUS PLAY method offers a number of opportunities for deep processing.

In step 2 of the LEGO SERIOUS PLAY Core Process, the participants build and give meaning to their LEGO models. Here, they have time to access and evaluate the meaning of what they are building—a course of action that Davachi, Kiefer, Rock, and Rock in the *NeuroLeadership Journal* refer to as "semantic processing."[2] This is what you did while building your model in the previous chapter.

In step 4—the reflection phase—other participants have the opportunity to ask questions of the model; this helps them access the meaning and allows the builder to elaborate. Your listener may have done this for your model of the aspect of your work that motivates you in the previous exercise. Typically, the facilitator will also ask questions and encourage the builder to tell the story from different perspectives.

Finally, in Application Techniques 2 to 7—where participants are cocreating models and stories—they tend to develop a deeper sensory processing. The multimodular way of working may also stimulate several networks in the prefrontal cortex and lead to strong memory formation.

Importance of Context

Context can serve as a good cue to retrieve memory. Re-creating or coming back to a memory, a certain context helps us remember insights and decisions we made in that moment. This is because memory is essentially an interaction between encoding and retrieval—and we recall information best when encoding and retrieval situations match. This can be seen when, for example, war veterans return to a battlefield and then a number of memories come up, or in a somewhat simpler example when we revisit our holiday photos.

The LEGO SERIOUS PLAY method strongly encourages the group to bring their LEGO models from the workshop back to the office, preferably to each participant's office if the models are individual. This helps create context-dependent memory retrieval; seeing the model frequently has the power to imagine themselves back in the workshop, which will help them retrieve memories and thus act on the decisions they made.

Generation

Generation is a process by which the learner is personally involved in making new knowledge. The simple observation from neuroscience (which seems to make great sense) is that generating information leads to better retention than simply reading it. Ownership optimizes learning and creates long-term memory—an age-old truth that now is supported by what we can observe in the brain. Generation and levels of processing are very closely related; therefore, if you produce your own learning, then you are processing more deeply. In a simple version, this is seen when we write something down; we may never look at the note, but simply having written it helps us remember.

The link to LEGO SERIOUS PLAY is that the process always starts with uninterrupted individual building of a LEGO model and story, and you will always have time to build *your own* answer to any question asked during step 1 in the Core Process. If or when there are follow-up questions during step 4 in the Core Process, these will cover topics in the already-built model, and will therefore lead to the aforementioned deeper processing.

Emotions

Research shows that there is a strong correlation between the "vividness of a memory and the emotionality of the original event."[3] The current thinking is that strong emotions help in two ways: (1) to focus the attention and (2) to activate a brain structure called the amygdala, a part of the brain thought to play a very significant role in everything related to controlling, experiencing, and coding emotions. Neuroscientists believe that if the amygdala registers something as emotional, it will signal to the hippocampus—which, as you recall, serves as the search and save engine—that "This memory is important, so you'd better save it so that we can find it again."

It is hard to imagine the LEGO SERIOUS PLAY method without emotions—mostly positive, but sometimes simply emotions. The play experience in itself creates a good mood, and the use of metaphors and stories creates strong feelings in participants—all of which help cement the process of remembering important elements. This could, for example, be something like "slaying the cash cow" in the example shown in Figure 7.1.

FIGURE 7.1   Slaying the Cash Cow

MEMORY AND ATTENTION: TWO MORE OBSERVATIONS

We have looked at some of the ways we can use the LEGO SERIOUS PLAY method to create the strongest possible memory formation and retention. We know that if you divide your attention, the resulting memory is weaker and more easily lost.

Thus, we aim to prevent participants from dividing their attention. Some research indicates that the hippocampus actually shuts down when this happens, which leads to little or no memory formation. Participants will not remember what has been said, what insights they unlocked, and what new decision came out of breaking their habitual thinking.

This leads us to two other memory-enhancing techniques that are used in the LEGO SERIOUS PLAY method:

1. *Distributing the learning over time.* This is used when iterating and revisiting individual models (Application Technique 1) and in particular when returning to

and creating landscapes (Application Technique 3). Designing a workshop that makes this possible helps distribute learning over time, which research has shown helps form stronger memories.

2. *Chunking.* The creation of LEGO models of complex issues can be seen as a way of simplifying and "chunking" knowledge. Similarly, we can view the landscaping technique—AT 3, where individual models are placed in a way that form clusters of similar meaning and a pattern of understanding—as a way of chunking. (See Figure 7.2.)

Simplifying and chunking also help to develop and store more information in our working memory and thus create deeper conversations.

FIGURE 7.2 **The Position of Each of the Models in Relation to Each Other Has a Meaning and Forms a Bigger Narrative**

DEVELOPING INSIGHT

In the previous chapter, we mentioned the outburst we hear so often during workshops: "I had no idea I knew this." But we only partly explained how this insight was formed. Here, we will look at additional explanations for where insights like these come from, and consider what the brain seems to require for insights to emerge and how they are present during LEGO SERIOUS PLAY.

Insights are essentially fresh knowledge that comes in the form of new and often surprising solutions, often to a known problem. Insights typically do not follow from an analytical process where we break down what we know into parts and then put it back together. Solving a problem using insights requires cognitive restructuring and reinterpreting one's view of the problem. Insights are typically surprising and feel like a eureka moment. In the Scurri case example in Chapter 1, one such insight came when the company realized it had been focusing on the wrong customer segments.

Insights are important because people tend to remember them better and more clearly than purely analytical solutions.[4] Strong declarative memory formation is a consequence of the perfect cocktail of an insight, close attention, and a balanced release of neurotransmitters called catecholamines.

Quieting Down

Scans have shown that the brain quiets down just before an insight occurs. There are fewer signals coming in and fewer signals between different brain waves. It has also been noted that the *wavelengths* of the signals change.

Therefore, the method allows for moments for the brain to quiet down. This typically happens during step 2 in the Core Process, in the construction phase. There is often a moment where the participant feels he or she is done building an answer to the question, but there is still time left. The participant relaxes during this moment, and we might hypothesize that the brain is quieting down and preparing for an insight. Indeed, there's often a second burst of energy and rebuilding.

Or rather this is what *used to* happen. Increasingly—and unfortunately—we find that rather than turning inward and integrating subtle signals in this moment, participants often turn their attention toward their smartphones, and lose whatever potential insight is to come. As facilitators, we encourage participants to stay focused; but most have become conditioned to use any moment of nonactivity to check e-mails or social media. Many organizations have some very unhealthy and brain-unfriendly working patterns when it comes to demanding that their employees be constantly "on." While that in itself could be the topic of another book, it's discouraging to think of all the potential insights we lose by giving in to this temptation.

"Occupy ACC"

In the moments leading to an insight and before the quieting down of the brain, there is increased activity in a brain structure called the anterior cingulate cortex (ACC). This structure, almost like the hippocampus, is highly connected with other brain regions, and is involved in many of the components of attention that we have touched on: memory, emotions, and also motivation. However, it also plays an important role in error detection and suppression.

Therefore, it seems crucial that this brain region not be occupied with or distracted by other demanding activities like suppressing emotions. This is why we try to get everything into the model in LEGO SERIOUS PLAY, and we make it clear that there is no wrong approach or solution. Encouraging participants to make everything concrete and visual gives them the opportunity to label what is on their minds—and keeps them from suppressing anything in the ACC.

Good Mood/Positive Affect

A positive mood makes it more likely to solve a problem with an insight—and thus more likely to form a strong memory. It puts the brain in a so-called preparatory state, possibly by better preparing the aforementioned ACC to detect new associations that it might otherwise have filtered out. Detecting these signals leads us to the final prerequisite in developing insights.

Attending to Subtle Signals

It is critical to allow LEGO SERIOUS PLAY workshop participants to have the quiet time that not only is necessary for memory formation, but also allows for the sensory gating wherein the brain shuts down against disturbing signals, in particular many of the visual inputs. In these moments, the brain turns inward and pays attention to some rather subtle signals coming from other parts—heeding signals that it might typically ignore.

A burst of gamma waves can be observed in the brain as it turns inward in this way. These waves have a different length than those we usually see, which has led neuroscientists to assume that their job is to help weave together the weak signals from different areas, thereby leading to the insight. One way to see the bricks and quiet time while building and interacting is as such variables.

Suspending Priming

Finally, starting with diversity in answers is an essential quality in developing insights and surprising solutions. But as we discussed in Chapter 1, the structure of the conversation in most 20/80 meetings leads to the first person speaking almost exclusively, and sets the frame for the solution. This is called *priming* in neuroscience; what happens is that we become anchored in that mode of answering. And it almost conditions us to keep answers and ideas with a certain realm, thereby limiting them.

LEGO SERIOUS PLAY can help suspend priming, since everyone always starts by building *one's own* model (specifically, in Application Technique 1). This allows all participants to develop answers without contamination from other people, and to create stories all their own.

Having looked at the brain, we will now turn to a theory that looks into the emotional feedback mechanism that helps us learn: flow.

CHAPTER 8

Flow—The Joy of Effective Learning

As mentioned in the introduction to Part II of this book, we see learning as making sense of an experience and incorporating that into our own mental models. It so happens that nature has equipped us with a special type of biological feedback that rewards appropriate learning activities (i.e., activities that serve to ensure our survival). Of course, survival for modern human beings largely means learning effectively in a meaningful context. Nature has arranged it so that we are rewarded with a deep feeling of enjoyment and satisfaction when we achieve this. We experience this feeling when we succeed, for example, with an interview for a job we really would like to land. The bigger the challenge seemed ahead of the interview, the bigger the reward in terms of a feeling of not only pleasure, but satisfaction.

This good feeling with which the body rewards us when we learn something important is the one of the most important driving forces in our development and understanding of the world. The body uses positive emotions and sensations to encourage us to learn what is important for us, since effective learning has been aiding us in our struggle to survive since the Stone Age. As mentioned in Chapter 7, the emotional reward drives our attention, which drives our learning, which drives our memory.

Over the past 30 years, countless researchers and scientists have thoroughly investigated this sense of deep satisfaction. One of these individuals is Hungarian psychologist Mihalyi Csikszentmihalyi, who refers to these feelings or this mental state as *flow*. The *flow* science is fully integrated into the LEGO® SERIOUS PLAY® method as the key learning driver both for the individual as well as for the group. It is impossible to imagine that the LEGO SERIOUS PLAY method would work without the LEGO bricks—or without integrating the *flow* concept.

Flow is a condition in which we are completely engrossed in a game or task, lose our sense of time and place, and utilize our learning potential to the fullest. The model presented in Figure 8.1 is a graphic representation of the flow concept.

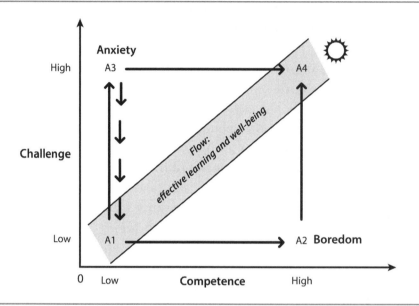

FIGURE 8.1   The Flow Concept
Source: Hans Henrik Knoop, *Play, Learning and Creativity: Why Happy Children Are Better Learners* (Copenhagen: Aschehoug, 2002).

The model illustrates how we arrive at the condition for flow when our competence and the challenge we face are in balance with each other. It also conveys how a lack of challenge leads to boredom and how facing too difficult a challenge creates anxiety. Finally, the model illustrates how we develop and become more competent as a result of experiencing flow; that is, we have a high point experience. A high point experience is when we succeed mastering a challenge that initially felt too hard and out of reach. It is when we surpass our own expectations to our abilities.

Let us walk you through the model. If we are in an A1 (lower left) or A4 (upper right) state—or anywhere on the diagonal corridor in between the two—our competencies are perfectly matched by the challenge. As a result, our bodies will reward us with a positive feeling of accomplishment and we will experience flow. If the challenge is greater than the competence (A3—upper left), we will experience anxiety.

We have two choices here: to acquire skills in order to achieve the A4 state, or to attempt to lower the challenge and move back to state A1. However, it is often difficult to ignore meaningful challenges in practice once you have become aware of them. When the level of competence is higher than that of the challenge (A2—lower right), we will become bored and will seek greater challenges, in order to achieve the A4 state once again. It would be meaningless to try to return to A1 in this case; this would imply ignoring or unlearning skills already acquired, which would be pointless.

Designers of ski resorts and computer games apply this model all the time. As you're likely aware, the goal of numerous computer and video games is essentially to get to the next level. By nature, we are built to strive for being in the flow corridor and to develop new learning. This is a driving learning force for the player (or skier) that the person aims to tap into. If you continue playing at level A1, you will eventually get bored and lose interest in the game—*unless* there is option of increase the challenge/level of difficulty so you can strive for an A4 state. If, on the other hand, the game's entry level is *too* challenging, you'll remain stuck at A3. You'll likely lose interest and move on to something else.

Those of you who have experienced downhill skiing will also recognize the flow model approach. The steepness and difficulty of the slopes are classified in levels from very shallow/easy to very steep/difficult with a system that is commonly known to skiers. We refer to these levels as green, blue, red, and black; green is the easiest slope and black the most challenging. This steepness progression enables you to learn effectively by choosing the context that fits your competence. Then, as your competence grows, you can also increase the challenge and achieve a state further up in the A1 to A4 flow corridor.

Whether you're playing a computer game or skiing downhill or completing a project for work, becoming totally immersed in the activity leads to a feeling of enjoyment and satisfaction as a result of getting better at the activity in which you are engaged. This process of getting better is a learning outcome—and it's crucial to understand that there is a *close connection between learning and flow*. This is best illustrated by comparing answers to two central questions. If you ask people when they feel they are able to learn most effectively, very few will answer that they find boredom—the

A2 state—instructive in the long run. Likewise, few people would claim that being in a state of anxiety (A3) enhances their ability to learn. While short periods of tension or anxiety may be necessary when starting on a task, they have a negative impact on learning over an extended period. The overwhelming majority of individuals will recall successful learning experiences during which they were sufficiently challenged by a task that really meant something to them. Thus the state of flow arises when the context is meaningful to us, and when our environment enables us to become fully involved in a task that neither bores us nor creates anxiety.

If we were then to shift our focus and ask when a person enjoys life most, we would find a similar pattern. Relatively few people would report that they enjoy life when they are bored; nor would many claim to like living in a state of anxiety. The vast majority would say that they are happiest when they are doing something that is neither too easy nor too difficult. By comparing these two factors, it is reasonable to conclude that enjoyment and learning are two sides of the same coin. We can see how both children and adults appear to be happiest when they are learning most effectively; we can even go as far as to assert that effective learning is experienced as playful, where play is considered broadly as the preferred mode of human being.

FLOW AND THE LEGO SERIOUS PLAY METHOD

You might recall from the Introduction to this book—where we described the development of the LEGO SERIOUS PLAY method—that something did not click in the early experiments that Johan Roos and Bart Victor conducted on using LEGO bricks for strategic development with executive teams in, among others, the LEGO Company. Later, we talked about cracking the code when referring to development by Robert and his team when they took over the further development of the method, and continued using it with teams in in a number of different companies and industries.

Both of these things (*not clicking* and *cracking the code*) indirectly refer to the *flow* concept. According to Hans Henrik Knoop (*Play, Learning and Creativity: Why Happy Children Are Better Learners*):

We have most fun, learn the most and are most creative when what we are doing is sufficiently difficult, because our entire being understands how to achieve its goals [when we're in] this situation. These goals include developing competence, vitality and complexity—and our brains react with positive emotional feedback, to encourage us to continue doing this.[1]

Once we appreciated the full consequence of the flow insight and made it the focal point for the LEGO SERIOUS PLAY operating system, things began to work. We knew we had a method that would greatly increase the chance that real changes and long-term learning would take place.

In practical terms, one of the first things that was codified was the use of *skills building*. Making these exercises an integrated part of the experience for all new LEGO SERIOUS PLAY users guaranteed that they would build competencies with the bricks and in the use of metaphors and stories. It also ensured that these competencies would be so high that they could face increasingly difficult challenges—another element that reflects an intentional use of the flow theory.

Participants who have completed a workshop with the LEGO SERIOUS PLAY method often describe their experience as an intellectual and emotional roller-coaster ride, and express a deep feeling of accomplishment. They feel that they and their abilities have been stretched, that time flew, and that it was an intensely enjoyable experience. What they describe is their journey through the flow model with multiple crossings in and out of the A1 to A4 flow corridor (see Figure 8.1).

However, each individual's road to this state of flow is different. Some in the group will feel anxious (A3) at the start of the workshop. Often these people will assume that the competencies needed to engage in the LEGO SERIOUS PLAY process are too high for them; perhaps they've never played with LEGO bricks before and fear that this will be a drawback. They may also assume that this is an undertaking that requires creativity, and if they do not consider themselves creative, this makes the perceived challenge very great.

Others in the group will allow themselves or expect to feel bored (A2). This group tends to assume that LEGO SERIOUS PLAY is frivolous or children's play only; they may perceive it as not appropriate or even as harmful for serious business.

Consequently, they feel that they are wasting their time by engaging in the activities. Both the anxiety (A3) and the boredom (A2) groups focus their attention on their expectations or misperceptions of the process in which they are about to engage, rather than concentrating on the workshop's objectives and purpose. Neither of these groups are looking forward to the experience.

The third group in the room is at A1 right from the beginning. They are looking forward to what is coming, in a state of readiness for optimal learning moving up the flow corridor toward A4.

This is where the aforementioned skills building becomes essential. One of the most critical skills for a successful LEGO SERIOUS PLAY facilitator is the ability to help the A3s and A2s move to the A1 state before the first 45 to 60 minutes have passed from the start of the workshop. The workshop's design, along with the progression and formulation of the challenges, has to help these groups move into the flow corridor. This movement and the succeeding climb through the optimal learning mode can happen when:

- Participants can focus on a task with clear goals.
- There is an appropriate balance between the challenge and the skills.
- They feel the right amount of stretch in terms of increasing challenges.
- The rules are clear and easily understandable.
- There is clear information on how well they are doing every step of the way.

This A1–A2–A3 mechanism can also be observed on a daily basis in most organizations. People who feel stressed, burned out, or just overwhelmed typically are in an A3 position and not able to acquire the necessary competencies or reduce the challenge sufficiently for them to experience more enjoyment and satisfaction with their job. Employees in the A2 stage will begin to look for new opportunities or feel that their performance is not been valued as it should be. Entire groups can begin to behave in similar ways. The responsibility for a good leader or manager is to continuously heed where his or her subordinates are in relation to the flow corridor and support their journey toward the never-ending A4 state.

In the next chapter, we will look at imagination: the mental power that helps us to see what is not.

CHAPTER 9

Imagination—Seeing What Is Not

Throughout history, the term *imagination* has had many different cultural and linguistic connotations. All share the basic idea that humans have a unique ability to form images or to imagine something, not only to mirror reality but also to transcend it. Imagination is our *mental capacity to conceive of what is not*—an ability that's central to the LEGO® SERIOUS PLAY® method. It's part of our goal to make people lean forward, unlock new knowledge, and break habitual thinking—all of which we want them to apply to enterprise, team, and personal development. LEGO SERIOUS PLAY should allow people to discover new realities and possibilities—in psychologist John Dewey's words, "to look at things as if they could be otherwise."

People often use the terms *imagination* and *creativity* interchangeably; however, this is imprecise at best or incorrect at worst. They are related, of course; if imagination is the ability to conceive of what is not, then creativity, in turn, is *imagination applied*. For example, members of a company are using their imaginations if they are trying to come up with ways to become more competitive in the marketplace. They are acting creatively when they actually *do* lower their prices and change their customer service because they have applied their imaginations.

Countless books and publications have been written about imagination. In the context of LEGO SERIOUS PLAY, the term implies not one, but at least three meanings:

1. Describing something existing
2. Creating something new
3. Challenging something existing

In LEGO SERIOUS PLAY we refer to the interplay between these three kinds of imagination as strategic imagination. But before we go further into that, let us go more in depth with the three roles of imagination—ways of forming images of what is not—since each is akin to a way of applying one's imagination.

DESCRIPTIVE IMAGINATION: MAKING SENSE OF THINGS

The role of descriptive imagination is to evoke images that describe a complex and confusing world out there. This is the imagination that rearranges data and information, identifies patterns and regularities in the mass of data that rigorous analysis generates, and is informed by judgment based on years of experience. Descriptive imagination not only reveals what is happening; it also enables us to make sense of it and to see new possibilities and opportunities. This need (and ability) to mirror the world is central in any kind of development, including enterprise development. For instance, Michael Porter's five industry forces, value chains, and the ubiquitous 2×2 matrices all invoke our descriptive imagination. Using metaphors such as landscapes to describe the world in different ways helps us to expand our descriptive images. This is the way that humans typically deal with confusing or complex information; by adding structure to information, we are effectively using descriptive imagination to focus on repeating patterns, and to see things in a new way. Alexander Osterwalder's popular Business Model Canvas is another example of using our descriptive imagination to make sense of the world (see the Scurri case in Chapter 1 for an example of a workshop based on the Business Model Canvas). The Weather Channel also makes extensive use of descriptive imagination to show us charts and diagrams to make its communication more effective. The image in Figure 9.1 is an example of using our descriptive imagination to illustrate the quality of leadership in a team. In this case there is only one correct way of thinking, which is the thinking that is identical to the leader's thinking.

CREATIVE IMAGINATION: CREATING SOMETHING NEW?

Creative imagination allows us to see *what isn't there*. It evokes truly new possibilities from the combination, recombination, or transformation of things or concepts. It is the essential feature of visioning, so-called skunk works, brainstorming, and thinking outside of the proverbial box. Whereas descriptive imagination enables us to see what

FIGURE 9.1   Using Your Descriptive Imagination to Represent the Uniformity in a Team's Thinking

is there (but in a new way), creative imagination allows us to see what isn't there (yet). We use this approach to create something really new and totally different. The image in Figure 9.2 illustrates an example of using our creative imagination. It might not be a good idea to have a fourth wheel that is larger than the others, but it is an example of seeing what is not there yet.

Creative imagination is associated with innovative strategies companies have undertaken not only to beat their competitors, but to make them totally irrelevant. It is in the spirit of what Gary Hamel—one of the world's most influential business thinkers according the *Wall Street Journal*[1]—calls "Competing for the Future."[2] Creative imagination was at work when Apple developed the strategy of iPads and iPhones and when companies like Google with Google Glasses, Virgin Group with Virgin Galactic, and Microsoft with Xbox extended their brands to new products and new markets such as consumer goods, space tourism, and games.

FIGURE 9.2   Using Your Creative Imagination to Show an Idea Not Yet Seen

People are motivated to call upon their creative imaginations when they are dissatisfied with current choices. Often cloaked in mystery, the creative imagination is at times described by such terms as *thunderbolts, God-given talent,* or *genius.* However, more sober minds find this imagination everywhere and in everyone—and realize that far from being mystical, it results from either an insight or a lot of experience and analysis. A famous example of creative imagination is the invention of the Rollaboard, shown in Figure 9.3.

The Rollaboard was invented in 1987 by Robert Plath, a Northwest Airlines 747 pilot and avid home workshop tinkerer, who affixed two wheels and a long handle to suitcases that rolled upright, rather than being towed flat as had been the case since the invention of the four-wheeled models.[3] His ability was to see what was not there yet within the area of luggage with wheels. The four-wheelers had been around since 1970, but had never really caught on.

Creative imagination takes a central role in the strategy process, and is often associated with innovative strategies. However, there is a clear division between creative imagination, where one focuses on possible realities and the making of reality,

FIGURE 9.3   Rollaboard

and fantasy, the domain of the impossible. When the creative imagination is taken to a negative extreme, we risk indulging in fantasy, the impossible, and the improbable. Strategy makers who lose touch with their experience risk fantasizing.

CHALLENGING IMAGINATION: CHALLENGE AND DESTRUCTION

Challenging imagination is completely different from the other two kinds. It is with challenging imagination that we negate, contradict, and even destroy the sense of progress that comes from the descriptive and creative imagining. Challenging imagination overturns all the rules and wipes the slate clean. It goes beyond creative imagination in that it does not merely add on a new element to what's already there;

FIGURE 9.4   Using Your Imagination to Challenge Conventional Wisdom

it completely dismantles what is there. It starts from scratch and assumes nothing. The image in Figure 9.4 illustrates an example of using your imagination to challenge the notion that wheels on cars have to be round. This forces you to come up with solutions for how you can make it pleasant to ride in a car with square wheels.

Some methods of challenging imagination include deconstruction and sarcasm. One potent example is engineer and management author Michael Hammer's notion of "reengineering." This notion—one that's frequently misunderstood—is not about improving existing practices. Rather, it is about "throwing it away and starting all over; beginning with the proverbial clean slate and reinventing how you do your work."[4] The challenging imagination was necessary at Nokia when the company left behind its tradition of wood products and rubber boots to become a telecom innovator—and it was also essential in the turnaround of the LEGO Company.

Though it might sound unusual, deconstruction in this sense is often paired with sarcasm and the recognition that there is no sacred thing as the "truth." The most popular manifestation of this approach is the comic strip "Dilbert." Creator Scott

Adams's parody of the business world has become a vital force within conversations among strategy makers across industries throughout the world. Of course, one can take this deconstruction too far and negate and reject everything, leaving oneself with nothing. The trap or pitfall of challenging imagination, then, is a kind of strategic nihilism, in which all choices are considered flawed, all plans unfeasible, and all positioning imprecise and deceptive.

STRATEGIC IMAGINATION

We've discussed how all humans have the ability to form images or to imagine something.

The challenging part, of course, is how to put this ability to work and *stimulate the creation* of these images. Imagine sitting around a table staring at a blank piece of paper or an empty whiteboard, being tasked with producing images that describe both what your business is today and what it should look like in the future. This is not an easy task for our imagination; it needs *tools* to work with. Let us look at an example of how the LEGO SERIOUS PLAY method helps our imagination.

The company that created the model shown in Figure 9.5 believed it had a unique new product invention (symbolized by the panda in the center); however, the new invention wasn't selling. The LEGO SERIOUS PLAY workshop uncovered the root problem: while the company was very proud of its invention (the triangular house in the middle housing the panda), it was afraid of copycats. Therefore, it was far *too* protective of its idea, which is conveyed by the fact that the panda is in a cage, surrounded by fences, with the team members acting as guards. They could see the customers (in the glass hut/dome) and the customers could see them, but the two couldn't communicate.

Once the team members understood the root problem, the marketing department played what-if games—in other words, conducted some scenario testing. They asked: what if we remove the guards and the fences? By envisioning and playing out potential consequences, team members were able to decide the best way to get the panda outside of the protected environment and into customers' hands.

FIGURE 9.5   Applying Strategic Imagination to Make Sense of the Situation, See What Is Missing, and to Challenge Your Current Way of Seeing the World

We can clearly see strategic imagination at play in this simple example—that is, the process that emerges from the complex interplay among the three kinds of imagination. LEGO bricks help participants apply their *descriptive imagination* to make sense of what is going on right now, then use their *challenging imagination* to form images of how they could change this situation, and finally, employ *creative imagination* to create the new scenario for moving forward.

We emphasize both the value and the danger of each of the three kinds of imagination, because we have found that most people tend to view imagination as the product of only the creative imagination and as being only positive. But each kind has its benefits and its drawbacks. While most people view the challenging imagination as being wholly negative due to its social effects on group interactions, it can also provide tremendous imaginative power. This supports the importance of the facilitator's role in creating space for the expression and positive benefits of each of the three types, while being sure to discourage the common negative social effects.

Workshop participants are not consciously aware of this interaction among the three kinds of imagination, nor is it directly observable. What we *can* observe are the manifested social dynamics among the participants in a LEGO SERIOUS PLAY workshop, which fall into three categories:

1. The construction of new knowledge gathered from knowledge and experience
2. The sharing of meaning emerging from that new knowledge
3. The transformation when assimilating the new knowledge

In the next chapter we will look at play, in particular serious play, and make it clear how the intentional use of imagination is an integral part of play.

CHAPTER 10
Play Is about Process

Back in Chapter 3, we briefly discussed our definition for serious play within the LEGO® SERIOUS PLAY® method. This chapter expands upon that definition in two ways: (1) by taking a closer look at the benefit power and purpose of play, and (2) by showing how the serious play characteristics come to life during a LEGO SERIOUS PLAY workshop.

THE BENEFITS OF PLAY

Let's review Johan Huizinga's four-part definition of play from Chapter 3. As you might recall, play:

1. Is fully absorbing
2. Is intrinsically motivated
3. Includes elements of uncertainty or surprise
4. Involves a sense of illusion or exaggeration[1]

Play is about *process*; work is about *results*. The purpose of using the LEGO SERIOUS PLAY method is to produce results (i.e., building a better business) faster. It's helpful to keep in mind that play in general is not a waste of time; it serves a purpose and offers many benefits for the player, such as:

- *Biologically*. Play positively influences brain development. It's actually a two-way street, in that the brain shapes the play but play also influences the brain. As play activities become more complex, new neural networks are added to handle this complexity. Leading researcher in play Stuart Brown says it elegantly and powerfully: "Play is like a fertilizer for brain growth. It is crazy not to use it."[2]
- *Socially*. Play helps develop the calibration of one's emotional responses to the world's many unexpected and ambiguous events. It helps prepare for unanticipated interactions by fine-tuning coping skills and refining social competences. During play, you can take on different roles, cooperate, or argue. You can explore, challenge, disagree, and come to agreement. Many parents—especially parents of boys—are familiar with something called play-fighting. This is a kind of play that is seen by

many researchers as essential for developing social skills, including how to handle conflicts. Play makes us feel alive, and helps us discover new limits and new possibilities. Again, Stuart Brown encapsulates it well: "Play gives us the irony to deal with paradox, ambiguity and fatalism. It nourishes the roots of trust, empathy, caring and sharing."[3]

- *Learning and development.* Play helps us test our capabilities, rehearse, and hone our skills. In addition, learning and memory seem to be fixed more strongly and last longer when we learn something via play. Play is a context in which we feel safe to take risks without worry, where we can imagine the unimaginable without fear, and where we can realize the seemingly impossible without hesitation. As Stuart Brown says, "When we stop playing, we stop developing, and when that happens the laws of entropy take over—things fall apart."[4]

MORE ON PLAY

According to Whitebread and Basilio (both researchers at the University of Cambridge), "Play is ubiquitous in humans; every child in every known culture plays, and there is strong archaeological and historical evidence that this has always been the case since the emergence of human species."[5]

Whitebread and Basilio also point out that adults typically not only support children in playing but also engage in play themselves. Yet, even if we all play—and we all know what playing feels like—things become much less clear when we try to pin down theories and definitions about play, what it is, and what it does.[6] With this in mind, we will nevertheless introduce insights and findings about play here in an attempt to make sense of it.

Play involves the following characteristics and elements:

- Typically, it is culturally, temporally, and spatially marked. Where, when, and how are clearly defined—for example, by:
  - Freedom (you don't *have* to play)
  - Separation (the aforementioned marking of time)

- Nonproductive orientation (people aren't playing to produce goods)
- Rules (that help suspend reality, or normal real life)
- Fictitiousness (an awareness that the play is different from real life)
- It both explores and represents whatever the player experiences in his or her daily life; for example, children will often play out a recent experience. In the chapter about the LEGO brick we wrote about how children often would build something capturing recent experiences. In the digital domain, it is seen how children playing Minecraft will copy real-life experiences virtually.
- It has typically been broken down into a number of categories—for example:
  - Physical play
  - Play with objects
  - Symbolic play
  - Pretense/socio-dramatic play
  - Games with rules

The LEGO SERIOUS PLAY method adds a new category: serious play.

The first important observation to make about the rough outline is that play is a *transformative power*—something that we all intuitively use while in childhood, and ought to use in adulthood as well. Humans by nature continue playing beyond an age that's observed in other species. This extension of play into adulthood is believed to be the basis of what Whitebread and Basilio called the "flexibility of thought which underpins the astonishing problem-solving abilities and creativity of humans."[7] Unfortunately, we have observed that while it is in our nature to keep playing as we grow, adults often ignore or suppress the use of this transformative power.

Play exists somewhere between reality and unreality. It is a paradox because it both is and is not what it appears to be; and unlike real life, play can be turned off. In other words, a player can step out of and back into play. That is, one can decide to stop playing, solve a mundane task, make a call, rest, and then step back into the play activity. Play is a creative liberation from what is constrained by our real or ordinary lives, and as such it is more than rational. Johan Huizinga, whom we have previously quoted, pointed out that humans are more than rational because play is irrational.

This somewhat elusive nature of play makes it a double-edged sword: while it helps the player develop, it is perhaps also what makes some adults in contemporary organizations shy away from it. They wonder: how can—or why *should*—one allow oneself to spend time somewhere between reality and unreality?

Indeed, this is one of the paradoxes about play: clearly, we would argue that play is not a luxury. It's not frivolous and certainly not something that should be left outside the door when one goes to the office. Rather, it should be carried into the office—and the best possible way to do that is through the LEGO SERIOUS PLAY method's use of serious play.

APPLYING SERIOUS PLAY IN A WORKSHOP

The three benefits of serious play we emphasize help shape the LEGO SERIOUS PLAY experience and delivery. They are the cultural, temporal, and spatial markers of serious play in the method, and therefore what we will focus on here.

A LEGO SERIOUS PLAY Workshop Is an Intentional Gathering to Apply the Imagination

In order for an activity to be considered LEGO SERIOUS PLAY, it has to be very clear (1) why the group is meeting, (2) who is meeting, and (3) where and when they are meeting. None of these can be random.

That it is an intentional gathering means it does not happen coincidentally; the group is meeting *on purpose and with a purpose*. They know what they want to work on and the nature of the challenge; they just don't know what the solution is. Thus, they need to apply their imaginations to see what is not, play that out, and reach a solution that they can make real.

We have described the descriptive, the creative, and the challenging imaginations as the three roles of imagination (in Chapter 9). These roles are deliberately used in the workshops with LEGO SERIOUS PLAY. However, while the particularities of applying the imaginations typically are not explicitly explained, it is essential to make it clear that the meeting's purpose is to *apply the imagination*—and that attendees are to do so on a particular topic that they've agreed upon beforehand.

A clear and motivating "why" helps the players in a LEGO SERIOUS PLAY workshop concentrate. Our prefrontal cortex always strives to focus us on longer-term goals and plans. Therefore, to allow for concentration on serious play, it has to be clear what the goals are and how they align with longer-term plans—either the individual's or the organization's.

The second intentional choice is who meets. The LEGO SERIOUS PLAY method rests on the assumption that everyone can and want to do well, and that the solution is in the room. The facilitator is there to facilitate—not to give the solution. Hence, it is important to get the people who are part of the solution into the room. And in order to be part of the solution, you need to be part of the current situation (the problem). Therefore, the process for LEGO SERIOUS PLAY requires that the gathering includes the people who will later need the result to make better decisions—the ones with habitual patterns they need to break and with potential and knowledge needing to be unlocked.

The participants should not only *be* part of the solution; they should also *want* to be part of the solution. Play, including serious play, is intrinsically motivated. Participants may wonder in the beginning whether the LEGO SERIOUS PLAY method is the right way to solve the issue; but they should never wonder about whether a solution is worth seeking and creating in the first place.

For the LEGO SERIOUS PLAY method to work, the physical setting has to be chosen consciously, and the time and timing have to be clearly defined. These elements in particular help the play become absorbing. The decisions here include finding a table of the right size and sufficiently comfortable chairs, and making certain that it is possible to concentrate as no other activities are happening at the same time.

The Workshop Is Preparing and Exploring, Not Implementing

You've heard us say time and again throughout the book that play is about the process, and work is about the result. Though it's a little simplified, this is intended to highlight how the play helps us *get to the solution*, and work is about *putting the solution to use.* This second part, work, often occurs via the implementation of a plan. Paradoxically, this also means that even though the delivery from a workshop with LEGO SERIOUS PLAY may be very concrete, it is primarily a preparation for making better implementation decisions, and through this building a better business. This process can be captured in the illustration in Figure 10.1.

FIGURE 10.1   The Goal of LEGO SERIOUS PLAY Is to Always Produce More Insight, More Confidence, and More Commitment

The Core Process of being asked a question, constructing an answer, sharing the answer, and reflecting on that answer leads to new insights about the topic that was asked about. This is the first part of exploring. Second, having unlocked one's own insights and heard all the insights from the other participants, this leads to more exploring and experimenting, taking the participants to a solution in which they have confidence. All of these insights have turned into something shared that everyone has confidence in, and then this leads to commitment, which means that when it is time to implement and make decisions the participants will actually do so—even when no one is checking on them.

For example, the process may lead to a new business model or a new vision; but neither of these by itself is the better business. Rather, they are *shared agreements* about how to make decisions moving forward. They will guide the management team about how to allocate resources, which markets to enter, or who to recruit. (See the case example 5 in Chapter 11 for an example of a company doing that.)

Another example is a LEGO SERIOUS PLAY workshop involving all the stakeholders in a new building construction project. The workshop can produce a comprehensive and shared design brief for the architects and engineers, but it doesn't produce the blueprint drawings themselves. The workshop's outcome will guide their decisions and build commitment to their work result. A LEGO SERIOUS PLAY workshop can produce the customer value proposition for a new product; but it does not produce the product itself.

Because participants don't feel pressured to directly produce and implement the final result, they are able to find LEGO SERIOUS PLAY safe, fully absorbing, and surprising—therefore improving the final quality of the delivery.

This takes us back to the zigzagging course we presented earlier in Chapter 4 (also see Chapter 11). You may remember how the zigzagging helped the participants reach their goal (their point B in the model), often in the shortest possible time. The zigzagging and speed are fueled by a process where the participants constantly imagine what the final result will look like, but are not making it as such (i.e., they are not responsible for directly producing anything). They are able to explore, experiment, and test without stress. In this way, the process often takes on *antifragile* qualities.

Essayist and scholar Nassim Nicholas Taleb defines antifragility as something that grows stronger through experiencing tests, challenges, and setbacks.[8] So anything created playfully explores what is possible and compels other participants to challenge it playfully.

As the LEGO SERIOUS PLAY process enters the phase where the delivery is taking shape, participants might engage in creating a landscape or a shared model, or in playing emergence—but even here they are kept in a serious play mode. Placing the models in relation to each other using Application Technique 3, creating a new shared model using Application Technique 2, or exploring how a system responds to an event using Application Technique 6, are not decisions. Instead, participants are *imagining and creating* new knowledge. When playing has led to a new state and a delivery has emerged, then the process can come to an end, and participants can document the delivery. You might recall our earlier example of the budget: when the budgeting process is done, then participants will record the budget in detail and use it to make decisions. Similarly, when a shared model building, for example, representing a new vision is done, then employees can record it, and use it for making their implementation decisions.

The example in Figure 10.2 visualizes the first step in documenting the results of the workshop. The photo records the key elements in an organization's aspirational identity. In addition to this there may be actions to take improving, strengthening, or otherwise altering these.

While the group is in the workshop, they can safely imagine what is not there, and they can explore, experiment with, and test these imaginary solutions since they're not under the gun to make something happen. This allows them to reach a shared solution and use a process that extends to better decision making in the future.

The Workshop Follows a Specific Set of Rules or Language

In order to support the process and protect the safe space in which play occurs, the LEGO SERIOUS PLAY facilitator will always define a set of very specific rules. Some of these are particular to the method and you'll likely recognize them from the LEGO

Improve the operational infrastructure and make that the centerpiece of the aspiration. Gear up the efforts to make the technical and support processes mesh more seamless and use this to drive the revenue growth (the treasure chest behind the gear wheels).

Set up a system that pumps all operation wisdom into a central knowledge database that is accessible to everyone in the frontline and maintained with a growth mentality (the plant on top of the person's head).

Start confronting both the living and dead "elephants in the room." Build a more trust-based organization that is less attractive for "elephants in the room."

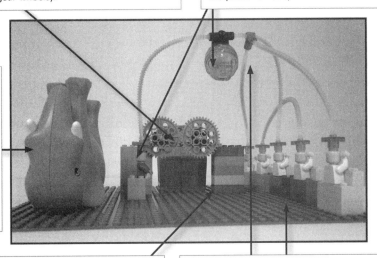

Protecting the frontline people with a solid wall from the distractions of the "machine room" and the potential elephants in the room.

Build a "one face to the customer" mentality driven by the same values (the identical head decorations) and nourished by a continuous flow of inspiration from the central knowledge base.

FIGURE 10.2   One Way of Recording and Communicating the Outcome of the LEGO SERIOUS PLAY Process

SERIOUS PLAY etiquette (Chapter 5), whereas others are well-established rules of facilitation.

Rule 1: The facilitator asks a question with many possible answers. It is clear and accepted that there is one person guiding the process, and he or she is asking the carefully crafted question. This facilitator may not have a particular power, status, or seniority outside the workshop; most of the time, he or she is not even part of the company itself. But this individual sets the direction during the process. This connects to the intentionality of the gathering: the intention is known and clear, and the participants trust the facilitator in this. Instead of challenging the facilitator's position and the right to ask that question, the participants have confidence in the process, and immerse themselves in exploring the answer.

Rule 2: Everybody builds and everybody shares. Everyone participates all the time in a LEGO SERIOUS PLAY workshop. Not only does this mean that nobody can sit on the fence and observe; it also means that each individual is expected to and will construct an answer to the facilitator's question with LEGO bricks.

Rule 3: The meaning is in the model, and the builder owns it. This also means that he or she *cannot be wrong*. Participants can expand ownership through the use of the landscape and shared model-building techniques; but everything starts on an individual level. This rule is typically rather easy for participants to follow. What they find more challenging is the limit it also sets; that is, if the meaning is the model, then *that* is what they share. Hence, one cannot go off on a tangent, let the mind wander, or bring in old arguments. If what they're addressing is not in the model, then it is not in the story—period. This helps keep the story not only emotionally engaging but also concise and not repetitive.

Rule 4: Questions are about the model—not the individual(s). Participants cannot interpret others' answers or claim that another person is wrong. They can *disagree*, which they can display through their own models or by using the question technique of *asking about the model*. This means that rather than asking a question directly to the person, the question is about what the person has built—what the participants can literally see. This way the serious play process takes the question out of the interpersonal domain and into the topic of the workshop.

In one workshop this truly helped the participants see eye to eye and move forward. It was a top management team who met to develop a new vision. The CEO was a newly appointed external hire, and among the participants at least three had harbored hopes of becoming CEO. There were lots of elephants and unspoken assumptions in the room, and only asking about what was in the models very much helped them move beyond looking at who was talking and listening instead to what was being said.

After an individual has shared his or her story the facilitator will demonstrate the technique of asking questions about the model, and also help the participants do the same (step 4, reflection, in the Core Process).

Rule 5: Mobile phones are off. Like all other play, serious play has to be fully absorbing, which participants can only achieve by turning off external disturbances. This practice typically is not allowed when at work or at leisure—but it's vital while at play, in particular serious play.

The topics of Part II—building knowledge, neuroscience, flow, imagination, and play—are each in their way pillars that support the LEGO SERIOUS PLAY method. As mentioned previously, some became part of the foundation early, and some emerged later as the method became clearer. Having described them in considerable detail, we will now turn to how the method has been put to work in organizations all over the world, and then in particular how it has been used in the LEGO Company. This is the focus of Part III.

LEGO® SERIOUS PLAY® at Work

Part III of this book will delve even further into how and where the LEGO SERIOUS PLAY method has been used for enterprise, team, and personal development.

We will start by describing the categories of challenges for which organizations typically use LEGO SERIOUS PLAY. We'll provide a specific set of examples, citing and describing where the method has been used across different industries and cultures. We will then give an overview of how it has been used *inside* the LEGO company as a tool for building a better business.

Our choices of examples in all cases have been guided by the desire to give you an impression of just how broad the application opportunities are.

While the method was developed to build better businesses, it is also being used outside business. We will give a short overview of these applications with special focus on education, from elementary schools to executive business programs.

Finally, we will bring the insights from these chapters together in a reflection on the art of designing workshops with the LEGO SERIOUS PLAY method, and conclude with a reflection on how it can help push boundaries.

CHAPTER 11

LEGO® SERIOUS PLAY® at Work in Business

Back in the Introduction to the book we the used a car metaphor for the LEGO SERIOUS PLAY method: LEGO SERIOUS PLAY can be a small car, an all-wheel-drive car, a limousine, or any other type. Now we want to share examples of the companies, teams, and individuals who have decided to "travel" using LEGO SERIOUS PLAY, where they wanted to go with the method, and why they chose to use this process to arrive at their destination.

This chapter is devoted to giving you actual case stories from a variety of industries and nonprofit organizations as well as government. We will share with you the insights we have accumulated over a 12-year period. We begin by giving you four bird's-eye lenses of how organizations have applied the LEGO SERIOUS PLAY method to develop their business, teams, and people. We will then present a number of actual cases and finish with some comments about the misconceptions regarding the application of LEGO SERIOUS PLAY, which we hope to dispel with this book.

BIRD'S-EYE LENS 1: THE MARKET USES LEGO SERIOUS PLAY TO GET PEOPLE TO LEAN FORWARD

The overarching goal for all applications is to build better businesses, better teams, and more competent individuals. In Part I, we described the need for going beyond 20/80, unlocking new knowledge, and breaking habitual thinking—a process shown in the diagram in Figure 11.1.

As mentioned, these may not be new needs for businesses. However, for competitive reasons and due to increasingly fickle yet sophisticated client and employee

FIGURE 11.1   Three Good Reasons for Using LEGO SERIOUS PLAY

demands, expectations have grown. It is not enough to have the experts leaning in, unlocking knowledge, and breaking habits; this process has to extend to everyone in the organization. LEGO SERIOUS PLAY users are drawn to the methodology because of its ability to go beyond the 20/80 syndrome and activate 100/100 participation. It gets everyone around the table involved and builds commitment to a sustainable and real improvement.

We can see these two kinds of interactions at odds in the photos in Figure 11.2. To the left, a typical situation in a workshop with LEGO SERIOUS PLAY, participants are all active; they are leaning in and contributing. On the right side, the often seen and more unfortunate normal meeting, one person is at the front of the room, next to the flip chart and with good control of the marker. The other participants in the meeting are leaning out, they are passive, and there may be even be a good chance that they are bored.

With the LEGO SERIOUS PLAY approach, the results are "lean forward meetings." This means more participation, more insights, more knowledge, more engagement, and, ultimately, more commitment and faster implementation.

FIGURE 11.2   To the Left a Lean Forward Meeting; To the Right a Lean Backward Meeting

BIRD'S-EYE LENS 2: THE MARKET USES LEGO SERIOUS PLAY FOR ENTERPRISE, TEAM, AND PERSONAL DEVELOPMENT

Let's review the model we have already shown once (in Chapter 4) to illustrate this (see Figure 11.3).

Some examples of personal development include coaching, conflict resolution, career planning, feedback for understanding of identity, and peer review conversations.

Team development is much more than team building: its goal is to directly address issues employees must tackle to make their team better and more effective. Consequently, it focuses on team members' identities and the team's visions, goals, strengths, responsibilities, processes, culture, and spirit, as well as strategies for improving performance.

Enterprise development covers all LEGO SERIOUS PLAY applications that are not specifically focused on team or personal development. Popular applications include organizational, business, and product development, as well as strategic planning, innovation, change and change management, mergers and acquisitions, education, and research. The hierarchy in terms of ordering and overlap in the model has a meaning. Enterprise development overlaps the other two ovals, followed by team development, with personal development in the background. The layering indicates that enterprise development is what the method is most often used for, but due to the

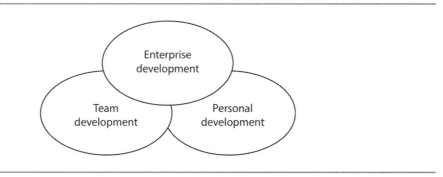

FIGURE 11.3   Enterprise, Team, or Personal Development

nature of the methodology there will always be a secondary default outcome in terms of team and personal development.

BIRD'S-EYE LENS 3: THE MARKET USES LEGO SERIOUS PLAY FOR COMPLEX, DYNAMIC CHALLENGES

One way of describing what we mean by *complexity* is that dealing with the challenge involves multiple stakeholders operating in a dynamic environment with a certain level of unpredictability. It is therefore impossible to move from A to B in a straight line, illustrated in Figure 11.4 as path 1 from A to B. We also referred to this in Chapter 4.

The organizations and managers who embark upon using the LEGO SERIOUS PLAY method often experience this challenge. It's not long before they find that trying to deal with complex challenges based on the assumption that you can make a detailed plan for getting from A to B in a straight and predictable line leads to a journey similar to the one in path 2, and not the intended journey in path 1. Their arrows end up pointing in all different directions; therefore, travelling on path 2 often means that the organization never arrives at the desired end state of B.

What is even worse is that some organizations try to adjust for this by outlining a new plan for going on a journey akin to path 1, but that rarely ends in success. And according to some, it falls under the very definition of madness: doing the same thing several times and expecting different outcomes. Instead of doing this, a group of

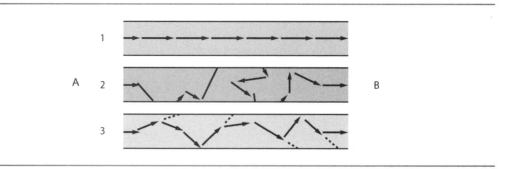

FIGURE 11.4 Different Ways of Getting from A to B

managers may decide to heed the complexity and unpredictability of the challenge by choosing to explore path 3 using the LEGO SERIOUS PLAY method. They accept that getting from A to B will be a zigzagging process—one that can be successful only if everyone is involved, everyone's knowledge is unlocked, and everyone's habitual thinking is broken. Once all these things are aligned, the team and the organization can begin navigating the challenging waters of complex issues.

BIRD'S-EYE LENS 4: THE MARKET USES LEGO SERIOUS PLAY TO BRIDGE DIVERSITY

There are trained LEGO SERIOUS PLAY facilitators and users in almost every corner of the world and in any kind of industry. The methodology works well within and across cultures, and it has been used on all continents, from an electronic giant in Tokyo, a big consultancy in the United States, a hospice in Copenhagen, and an NGO in Myanmar to organic farmers in New Zealand and small cattle holders in East Timor.

Often, the differences among people—due to factors like position, age, language, culture, education, competences, and background—can become obstacles for a group's ability to work together effectively to develop their business. Experience shows that the method not only transcends these differences or boundaries; the method also has the ability to turn this diversity into a benefit for the group.

If we look at which industries and organizations have used LEGO SERIOUS PLAY, we see a similar picture. It appeals to a broad range of industries and to large as well as small companies. It appeals to for-profit corporations, nonprofit organizations, and government institutions. We also find many users within the field of higher education.

EXAMPLES OF LEGO SERIOUS PLAY AT WORK

This section covers a number of diverse interventions with LEGO SERIOUS PLAY. Some we have designed and facilitated ourselves; others have been designed and delivered by facilitators we have trained and certified. Table 11.1 shows an overview of the examples and indicates their placing, either by chapter number or by case example number.

TABLE 11.1   Case Example Overview

	Large Companies	Small and Medium-Sized Companies	Government Organizations	Nonprofit Organizations
Enterprise Development	Pharmaceutical Company Building a New Manufacturing Site (#1) Creating Value Propositions for Strategic Business Units in a Multinational Chemical Company (#2) Concept Development for a Showroom (#3)	Architectural Firm Ownership Transition (#4) Internet Retailer Strategy Development (#5) Developing a Business Model at an Internet Start-Up (Chapter 1)	Future Scenarios in a Government Department (#6) Project Kickoff for a Multiple-Stakeholder Consortium (#7)	Strategic Partnership Development (#8)
Team Development	Building a Transformational Leadership Team at a Global Service Center (#9) Global Marketing Team in a Mining Company (#10)	Improving Communications in a Virtual Team (#11)	Team Workshop at an Embassy (#12)	Becoming the Best Possible Leadership Team at a Nursing Home (#13)
Personal Development	Developing Strategic Thinking Capabilities (#14) Personal Career Development Planning (#15)	Talent Development at a Medium-Sized Pharmaceutical Company (#16)	Refocus to Reenter the Labor Force (#17)	Muscular Dystrophy Association: Defining the Good Life (#18)

Case Example 1: Pharmaceutical Company Building a New Manufacturing Site

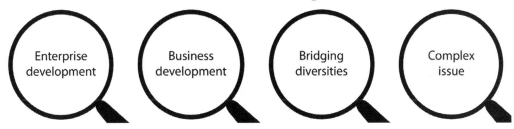

Enterprise development | Business development | Bridging diversities | Complex issue

Background: An international pharmaceutical company headquartered in Scandinavia planned to construct a new $200 million manufacturing facility in South America. It would be its largest ever—two to three times the size of its current facility. In addition, the company was going to have to build the facility faster than anything it had previously built.

Issue: Challenges included (1) developing a shared strategy for leaders who would be relocated with their families for a period of two to three years to oversee the project, (2) bringing the leaders together as a team on both personal and professional levels, and (3) integrating headquarters goals with the knowledge and insight of the South American team members.

LEGO SERIOUS PLAY intervention: The solution was a two-day strategy workshop for a group consisting of employees from the headquarters, the leaders to be relocated, and local leaders from the South American plant. The workshop was delivered by two facilitators.

Outcome: LEGO SERIOUS PLAY made it possible for the participants to see and understand the project's systemwide impact. This allowed team members to identify potential problem areas that were not obvious to them before the workshop. As a result, the plant was finished on time and within budget. In addition, one area they hadn't considered before engaging in the workshop involved practical concerns about how families would adjust to living abroad. In prior transitions like this one, many spouses became unhappy. So the company used LEGO SERIOUS PLAY once again with the families—and thanks to this, relocated families have happily adjusted to their new homes and have made many new friends.

Case Example 2: Creating Value Propositions for Strategic Business Units in a Multinational Chemical Company

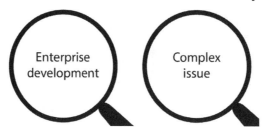

Background: The company is a well-known multinational corporation (MNC) present globally in a number of industries with over 100,000 employees, upwards of 300 production sites, and more than €60 billion in annual sales.

Issue: The organization was undergoing a change process: specifically, it wanted to help its engineers and strategic business unit (SBU) leaders to focus less on their products' features and more on the value delivered to the client. Traditionally, the company had delivered excellent products, thereby encouraging a strong engineering culture rather than a customer-focused culture in most units.

LEGO SERIOUS PLAY intervention: The workshops were tied into part of a larger process. Each lasted one day and included participants from the SBU management team and/or leading engineers. The participants built models of the SBU organizational identity followed by a landscape with models of the customer needs (i.e., Application Technique 3). The workshop concluded with developing a shared model telling the story of the value proposition.

Outcome: The groups left with the LEGO model, the recording of the story, and a first version of the value proposition in writing. This helped fuel the transition from a focus on features to value delivered.

Case Example 3: Concept Development for a Showroom

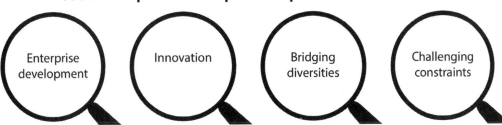

Enterprise development • Innovation • Bridging diversities • Challenging constraints

Background: In October 2011, Hitachi Electronics Services Co., Ltd and Hitachi Information Systems, Ltd merged to become one information technology (IT) services company known as Hitachi Systems, Ltd. A project team that consisted of members from the two previous firms was established immediately. This group's primary objective was to alter the concept they had used previously at their main office in Mita, Japan—a traditional showroom—and move toward a new "integration space" at Osaki. The new setup would allow customers and employees to hold meetings, seminars, and other events in more open and comfortable environments.

Issue: The team had to implement the concept by the summer of 2012. If they pulled off the development process well, it would become a symbol of the success of teamwork for members from two different firms. The project team members wanted to accelerate the project and also make their concept more obvious: to have a clearer image of the identity of the space, and to express how it was going to surprise and impress people.

LEGO SERIOUS PLAY intervention: A one-day workshop for a team of 12 to 15 people was conducted in Tokyo. Two facilitators split the team into three groups. Each participant created a room space identity model to convey his or her understanding of the meaning of *impressive* and *surprised*; they then collected and told stories of "the integration room of the future" by integrating the defined models. Each group made a presentation of the future space concept, identifying

(continued)

(continued)

the key value propositions that made up the full concept. Hitachi documented the entire process and outcome and used it to design the actual space in the following months.

Outcome: The new integrated space opened in the summer of 2012, and its success can be attributed to the feedback from the project. As expressed by one of the project managers: "The workshops gave us the ideas and key words [we needed] to develop into two concrete concepts in order to pass our ideas to our contractors-designers. The project team members from the two original entities also showed more respect toward each other during the session and [gave one another equal time to] express their ideas. Despite [the fact that we] came from two different [companies], we were able to commit to the outcome and implement the overall concepts [we gleaned] from the workshop."

Case Example 4: Architectural Firm Ownership Transition

Enterprise development

Strategic planning

Multiple stakeholders

Leaning forward

Background: The founders of a large U.S.-based architectural firm had passed the reins over to two senior architects who had been groomed to lead the firm.

Issue: The new leaders could see that shifting market demand and increased competition would require a radical change in the firm culture. In the past, the now-retired founders had been responsible for getting new clients, leading project design, and managing the firm. The new leaders envisioned a culture of market-focused shared leadership.

LEGO SERIOUS PLAY intervention: Together with the new leaders, the facilitator designed a one-day workshop to unearth the skeletons in the closet—that is, to distinguish the current firm from the cultural rules the founders had established. They were also seeking to help develop nine emerging leaders, and to begin to design and implement a market-focused culture of shared leadership.

Outcome: The workshop helped all participants to see each other in a new light. The two sponsors were able to assess their nine emerging leaders' interests and motivations, and the leaders themselves were able to form new bonds and also play an integral part in shaping the firm's future direction. The collective aspirations voiced during this workshop became the foundation for firm planning goals. During the workshop, employees formed subcommittees for each of four areas of focus—design, technology, marketing, and finance. These four committees became internal designers and advocates for change, allowing workshop participants to become stakeholders in the changes they designed together.

Case Example 5: Internet Retailer Strategy Development

Enterprise development   Business development   Complex issue   Multiple stakeholders

Background: This is a family-owned European Internet retailer working in three countries that operates under several brand names in these various countries. The company has grown significantly over the past couple of years, partly organically and partly through acquisitions. It sells mostly refrigerators, freezers, and electronics.

Issue: The board, consisting mostly of non–family members, had set a simple yet demanding goal for the company: within five years, double the top line and the bottom line. After receiving this directive, the CEO/owner and COO decided to contact the LEGO SERIOUS PLAY facilitators.

LEGO SERIOUS PLAY intervention: The entire process ran over six months with three separate two-day strategy workshops involving the following steps:

Interviews were conducted with a number of employees from various levels of the organization.

An initial workshop was held in the company's home country involving participants who were members of corporate top management and local upper-level managers.

Second and third workshops took place with the daughter companies; participants here were members from corporate management and country management.

Each workshop followed the same design: the participants built model(s) showcasing the company's current situation, the strategic landscape (clients and other stakeholders and the connections between them), the aspiration for what the company could become, and what the focus areas should be.

Last, they rated these focus areas. In one or two of the workshops, participants also played out a few events in the landscape (Application Technique 6).

The COO and CMO formed a task force using the facilitators as sparring partners, where they compiled, compared, and rated focus areas, which they later quantified and analyzed. They eventually decided to concentrate on a subset of these areas, which they elaborated further.

Finally, they gave a presentation to the board. The task force and one of the LEGO SERIOUS PLAY facilitators presented the process and results to the board, and it was decided to prioritize three of the focus areas.

Outcome: The strategy is going into the second year, and the company is well on its way to fulfilling the targets. As a kickoff to the second year, a one-day ideation workshop (not LEGO SERIOUS PLAY) was conducted in order to come up with short-term activities that could support the focus areas.

Case Example 6: Future Scenarios in a Government Department

Background: The department, part of the Ministry of Social Affairs in a European country, was tasked with working in a highly polarized area that frequently commanded the general public's attention.

Issue: Due to the department's task and foreseeable challenges from elected politicians from both sides of parliament, the department wanted to create a sense of a burning platform and a strong set of actions. They wanted have a clear understanding of core values and how they could be more adaptive and resilient for the future.

LEGO SERIOUS PLAY intervention: The LEGO SERIOUS PLAY facilitator designed a two-day workshop based on scenario thinking as described by Kees van der Heijden and Adam Kahane (also mentioned in Chapter 3 as an example of play). The participants' objective was to build the department's core values and envision what it could become. From that they moved through creating model of possible yet extreme futures. In order to prepare themselves to create these, they first built models of driving forces—defined as underlying and typically unpredictable forces that shape the surrounding world and that impact the observable trends, for example the degree of centralization—and then ranked these according to impact and predictability.

Outcome: Imagining and building these extreme yet possible futures helped the department develop a set of actions that created a robust strategy framework. This, along with the clear articulation of the department's core purpose and vision, kept it focused on delivering value to a number of vulnerable or marginalized groups. The department secured its further survival and is still playing an important role in the welfare of special groups.

Case Example 7: Project Kickoff for a Multiple-Stakeholder Consortium

Enterprise development | Complex issue | Challenging constraints | Multiple stakeholders

Background: ICEMAR, a project established to monitor ice movement in Arctic waters, delivers existing sea ice information products directly to vessels operating in icy waters, and sought to ensure the sustainability of the service in the long term.

A consortium of partners from six different countries and composed of private companies and public service providers led by Kongsberg Satellite Services AS (KSAT), a Norwegian satellite services company and the world-leading company for maritime monitoring and surveillance systems, was tasked with developing ICEMAR as an integrated solution to increase the availability of ice information data on board vessels navigating near or in ice-infested waters in the European Arctic and the Baltic Sea.

Issue: The first phase of this project—funded by the European Union and with a very short time frame—was to develop and demonstrate a pilot sea ice information distribution system. The consortium members came from different countries and both private and public organizational cultures. They represented meteorological centers, software developers, and telecommunications and satellite image providers, among others.

KSAT assembled a project team of 15 people representing all members of the consortium to lead the development. They faced several challenges: very few of the members knew each other, only a handful were even aware of what the project was about, the task was complex with no precedents, the commercial interest varied among the consortium members, and there was an urgent need to get going with the actual work in order to meet the funding deadlines.

(continued)

(continued)

LEGO SERIOUS PLAY intervention: The project work began with a two-day workshop of which a day and a half were spent with LEGO SERIOUS PLAY. The goals of the workshop were to build a shared understanding of the nature and content of ICEMAR, to identify and prioritize the issues that the team needed to undertake in the first phase, and to create a positive spirit for the upcoming development.

Outcome: Over the course of the a day and a half, the team managed to accomplish the following:

- Define and specify the ICEMAR project content and create a shared vision that would serve as the guiding star from that day until the project was completed.

- Identify the scope of technical issues and process challenges the team would need to manage in both the short term and the long term, including prioritization.

- Transform from a group of individuals with different degrees of interest in the project to a team of dedicated and motivated experts working toward a common goal.

At this point in time, the project has been successfully completed, and the results live up to the outcome of the workshop.

Case Example 8: Strategic Partnership Development

Enterprise development · Multiple stakeholders · Strategic planning · Challenging constraints

Background: *FIRST* is an international nonprofit organization, headquartered in Manchester, New Hampshire, with a mission to inspire young people to be science and technology leaders by engaging them in exciting mentor-based programs that build science, engineering, and technology skills; inspire innovation; and foster well-rounded life capabilities, including self-confidence, communication, and leadership.

One program inspires younger students aged 9 to 16 (9 to 14 in the United States/Canada and Mexico) to solve real-world engineering challenges by building robots to complete tasks on a thematic playing surface and to complete a research project. The teams, guided by their imaginations and adult coaches worldwide, discover exciting career possibilities and, through the process, learn to make positive contributions to society.

A major partner in this program is the robots manufacturer since the availability of the educational robots in the classroom is a necessity for the program events, which in turn are essential for attracting a corporate sponsor to finance the events.

Issue: Due to a much higher interest worldwide for participating in the programs offered by *FIRST*'s distribution strategy, the organization had become a bottleneck for its own further growth as of 2008. It had begun with a limited scope, which had made it easy to maintain quality with the small team responsible for all aspects of both design and delivery. At that time, the setup was highly local and therefore not scalable for a global reach, which was the partnership's goal. This had resulted in a more overall strategic discussion about the long-term aspiration

(continued)

(continued)

for the program's identity, purpose, implementation, and scaling. The leadership team needed to revisit the original intentions, define the future direction, and get everyone to commit to this journey.

LEGO SERIOUS PLAY intervention: A one-day workshop with participants from *FIRST* and the partner was designed to achieve the following four goals:

1. Feel the pulse for the program partnership. Is it just fine, too hard, too rapid—or something else? Additionally, determine if there is a need for going to the doctor and prescribing some medicine.

2. Identify the essence of a program event regardless of where in the world it takes place.

3. Develop a clear picture of the shared expectations for the next three to five years.

4. Identify steps to implement the outcome of the workshop.

Outcome: The workshop fully met the goals set—and for the first time ever, both parties in the partnership fully understood and appreciated each other's positions. It turned out that their aspirations for the future growth and how to change to a more scalable distribution strategy were much more aligned than anyone had imagined was the case. As a result, the workshop revitalized the partnership and became the starting point for a new era—one in which the program grew from being local to being global in reach.

Case Example 9: Building a Transformational Leadership Team at a Global Service Center

Team development

Background: The client was a global network and communications company with three global service centers that support the entire organization. The center in Mexico City had been formed three years prior to our meeting with them, and had grown from 100 to 3,000 employees in that time.

Issue: The center was moving from providing bespoke to more standardized solutions. Management had realized, in the words of the center's top manager: "What drove us to grow will not keep us growing. We now have scale; next, we need to bring the value to organization, and that needs to come through a transformation—an industrialization of our services."

The purpose became to build a leadership team that could create and carry out transformation.

LEGO SERIOUS PLAY intervention: A one-day workshop was held with the leadership team, a total of 13 people with very diverse backgrounds and from different countries in Latin America. The participants started with building models of themselves, exploring their values, leadership strengths, and competencies. From this they moved on to exploring what characterized the team as a whole, the hurdles to transformation, and a vision for what they could become. The workshop closed with a reflection in which they moved backward from the vision to the current situation and identified initiatives in that process.

(continued)

(continued)

Outcome: The team developed a vision for themselves that included defining good leadership. Having defined hurdles to the transformation (e.g., lack of resources and employees wedded to the current status), and having identified what each them could bring out in themselves that would accelerate that transformation, they used this insight to kick off a robust transformation process.

Case Example 10: Global Marketing Team in a Mining Company

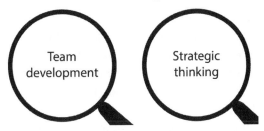

Background: The Eurasian Natural Resources Corporation plc (ENRC) integrates mining, processing, energy, logistics, and marketing operations. It originated as part of the privatization process in Kazakhstan in 1994, and in its present form was established in 2006 with headquarters in London. Its ferro-alloys global marketing team has its base in Zurich, but members are based in several locations in the Euro-Asian region. Because ENRC works with clients all over the world, it felt the implications of the recent global financial crisis. The year 2012 was especially challenging, according to Alex Tattersall, then ENRC's marketing director of ferro-alloys, who needed to align his team on common aims for 2013. They had developed corporate strategy; what they needed from employees were alignment and focus.

Issue: Tattersall, who has since left ENRC, wanted to start 2013 on a new and positive note by bringing his team together and on task in an environment of open dialogue. He wanted a process that could run his team through the business in a new way; therefore, he assigned two LEGO SERIOUS PLAY facilitators to do a one-day workshop with this purpose. As Tattersall explained, "We have a core team in sales as well as supporting functions such as human resources, IT, compliance, and quality assurance units. I wanted to create an alignment of the team—to make us think in the same way, to be better in terms of strategic clarity, communication with production plants, and leadership."

LEGO SERIOUS PLAY intervention: A one-day workshop for a team of 15 people was developed. The workshop was held off-site in a beautiful location in

(continued)

(continued)

Switzerland, with everyone arriving the night before. The team was split into two groups, each with their own facilitator. Each group developed their version of a team vision, specifying what kind of team it would take to live up to the goals the corporate strategy had set forth. The two groups shared their visions and agreed on next steps. During the process they also built models of what they saw as hurdles to executing the strategy.

Outcome: During the workshop, it became obvious to Alex Tattersall and his team that they had lacked clarity. The diversity of ENRC's operations had limited communication within the sales team. The workshop served to bring everyone together physically—and from there, they were able to come to a common awareness of where they most required improvement. By the end of the day, they had developed a shared vision of what the team should look like by the end of 2013—and thus, what kind of team it would take to execute the corporate strategy.

"Making everything concrete in the LEGO brick models created a relaxed atmosphere and made 'all noses point in the same direction,'" explains Alex. "I can honestly say that in this case the workshop itself was the benefit—no more, no less." He concluded: "We had fun while doing something serious."

Case Example 11: Improving Communications in a Virtual Team

Team development

Challenging constraints

Complex issue

Background: A medium-sized global communications technology company had organized its reverse logistic processes around three remote centers, all located in North America. The dispersed team—who got together only twice a year and worked in different time zones—was responsible for coordinating logistics nationally.

Issue: To be effective, team members needed to develop a deeper understanding of each other's critical success factors, understand how individual roles and responsibilities impacted team objectives, and function as an integrated team. Reliance on virtual communication further complicated the team's interaction.

LEGO SERIOUS PLAY intervention: The leader decided to bring the team together in a central location, and worked with a LEGO SERIOUS PLAY facilitator to design a workshop to improve group communication and productivity. The workshop clarified each team member's responsibilities, functions, and constraints, and the interdependencies among all the team members. Individual special strength models and team identity models were also constructed. Using the landscape they created a representation of the entire complex system that they were all part of, the team replayed a number of team breakdown situations and used their new team knowledge to play out various alternative responses. These scenario plays helped them understand how they could avoid misunderstandings and bad communication in the future.

(continued)

(continued)

Outcome: The workshop had a dramatic impact on the team's morale and productivity. In the words of the team leader, "We continued talking about the business scenarios after the workshop. My team wants to discuss a different scenario at each staff meeting, and they want to get together face-to-face once a quarter. The staff meeting will be much more about how we can help each other. Dinner that night was so different from the previous night. [It was as though] we had become a team overnight."

Case Example 12: Team Workshop at an Embassy

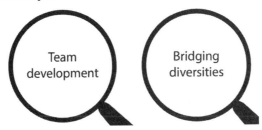

Team development

Bridging diversities

Background: The embassy, located in a Latin American country, is staffed with a mix of local and expatriate employees, a number of whom were recently hired. The ambassador heads the embassy, with the Deputy Head of Mission as second in command. The embassy represents a European country.

Issue: A VIP delegation, including a number of leading business people and dignitaries, were coming to the country for an official visit. Such visits are the moment for an embassy to shine; however, they also require detailed and demanding planning. Their intense nature stresses full execution: everything has to work smoothly. Cultural differences and varying experience only add to the challenge.

The embassy wanted to prepare for the unexpected in order to make better decisions if such an event happened.

LEGO SERIOUS PLAY intervention: A one-day workshop was conducted with the entire team—16 people in total. The team was split into two groups reflecting the day-to-day subgroups in which the employees would work. Each had its own facilitator, one local, the other from the European country.

Outcome: The group developed a set of Simple Guiding Principles (SGPs, Application Technique 7) that would help them make good decisions when the unexpected occurred. These principles would help employees act immediately and remain aligned so that an event or interaction they hadn't foreseen wouldn't throw them for a loop. The teams also articulated what kind of group culture they would like to maintain leading up to and during the VIP visit. In order to develop their Simple Guiding Principles and a better preparedness, they also played out a number of possible events that could happen during the visit.

Case Example 13: Becoming the Best Possible Leadership Team at a Nursing Home

Team development

Background: Two nursing homes in the same small town had just merged, creating a new facility. The new manager had led one of the two, and had just formed her new leadership team. Both homes had been run by the local government, and the merger had been an attempt to achieve better economics through economies of scale.

Issue: The intention was quite simply not only to form a leadership team, but to create the *best possible* leadership team. The new leader wanted to hit the ground running and eradicate any instance of an "us versus them" mentality between staff members from the previous nursing homes.

LEGO SERIOUS PLAY intervention: The LEGO SERIOUS PLAY facilitators designed a long one-day workshop where the participants built models of themselves, including elements like what they believed in and what they saw as their competencies. This was followed by building models of the kind of decision-making culture it would take to be the best possible leadership team. They then tested these cultural elements with Application Technique 6 where they played out various scenarios that might occur.

Outcome: Participants emerged from the session as *one* team, with a much deeper understanding of each other and an agreement on how to work together, thereby allowing the newly merged nursing home to start off with an immediate advantage.

Case Example 14: Developing Strategic Thinking Capabilities

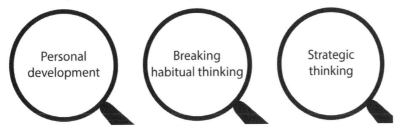

Background: The learning and development division within a global consulting company decided to develop a leadership development program focusing on helping participants to realize what essential qualities they need to master in order to achieve their ultimate goal. For them, the goal was to move from an end-to-end management style to a leadership style based on empowering, delegating, and thinking strategically.

Issue: The goals of the program were:

1. Enhance the participants' ability to think, communicate, and act strategically in a project leadership role (i.e., develop skills that would help them decide where to look, what to focus on, and how to act, while leaving the day-to-day course of action to their team).

2. Foster the participants' innovative capabilities, inspire them, and give them tools to challenge the current ways of thinking while not assuming that what has worked in the past also will work in the future.

3. Increase the participants' consultative skills by strengthening their facilitation, cocreation, and advisory skills with a focus on helping the internal clients uncover deeper knowledge and new value, rather than providing solutions and taking action for these internal clients.

LEGO SERIOUS PLAY intervention: Participants worked with LEGO SERIOUS PLAY over a day and a half to achieve these goals. During the process, they identified

(continued)

(continued)

what they considered to be the core characteristics of strategic leadership. They mapped out the landscape in which they planned to exercise this leadership in an imagined future. Based on this definition and landscape, they played out a number of scenarios that helped them hone their strategic thinking capabilities and take the mental leap from managing to leading. Finally, through each individual model gathering all their key insights from the entire workshop, the group extracted a set of Simple Guiding Principles (SGPs) that can guide their continued development after completing the training course. Here are some examples of the group's Simple Guiding Principles:

SGP: Get out of my own way.

SGP: Drive conversation; don't just respond.

SGP: Slow down and breathe.

Outcome: As a result, program participants are better equipped to take on more senior roles in the organization due to their ability to strategically lead their teams, clients, and projects. Of the first class of 15 participants, 10 received a promotion to the next level within six months. The company recently completed the program for the second time.

Case Example 15: Personal Career Development Planning

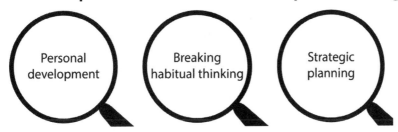

Personal development

Breaking habitual thinking

Strategic planning

Background: Hakuhodo, Inc. is a leading advertising and marketing consulting firm in Japan. The firm has been using LEGO SERIOUS PLAY since 2007 to enhance client cooperation.

Issue: In most Japanese enterprises, promotions of employees are related to their job performance and seniority. Under such circumstances, employees tend to base their career development on the firm's policy and plans. Hakuhodo wanted to develop a new career development program, where employees must plan for their future and take initiative to select their own career goals.

In 2010, the LEGO SERIOUS PLAY facilitators worked together with members of Hakuhodo University to develop a unique career development program in which LEGO SERIOUS PLAY would play a major role. The program targeted middle managers of Japanese firms, mostly Hakuhodo's client firms. Hakuhodo also wanted to apply the program to its own employees and support middle managers who had to choose a career path: to become either professionals with particular expertise or senior managers with their own teams. The program should induce self-motivation in participants, encouraging employees to consider their employer's long-term goals and mission in developing their own careers. The program was also aimed at guiding the participants' decisions about which proper steps to take to accomplish their career goals inside the company.

LEGO SERIOUS PLAY intervention: Hakuhodo University and LEGO SERIOUS PLAY facilitators underwent a number of pilot trials to complete the program

(continued)

(*continued*)

design. The entire career development program covered two and a half days, of which a LEGO SERIOUS PLAY workshop occupied one and a quarter day. The LEGO SERIOUS PLAY portion consisted of four factors:

1. Reviewing the participant's past
2. Imagining his or her future
3. Creating accelerators to boost him or her into that future
4. Uncovering obstacles that may keep him or her from reaching it

This was conducted by both external as well as internal facilitators.

Outcome: Hakuhodo has used the program, named CreateMe, both internally and with outside clients since 2011, and has enjoyed great success in doing so. The name reflects the idea that each employee, not the company, is responsible for his or her career workshop. The program has given wider career options to participants and given clients opportunities to openly discuss career options in earlier days of the participants' careers.

Case Example 16: Talent Development at a Medium-Sized Pharmaceutical Company

Background: Like many pharmaceutical companies, this medium-sized European player had experienced market changes in recent years. Its patents were running out, and the company's leaders were feeling increased pressure from low-cost and/or copycat products. One part of their answer was to increase focus on talent development, so they decided to launch a search for midlevel managers and talents as part of a 2010 initiative.

Issue: The company wanted to create an innovative process that encouraged employees to learn in a different way than the conventional teaching approach. They selected an experienced group of facilitators and the LEGO SERIOUS PLAY method for the task. The workshop would be part of a longer process, and serve as the main component in the module related to learning how to develop strategy.

LEGO SERIOUS PLAY intervention: A case was developed in collaboration with the client company where the case company was similar to yet sufficiently different from this particular pharmaceutical company. The participants received the case as preparation and then role-played being the management team; they then went through a session with LEGO SERIOUS PLAY, which helped them in developing the new strategy and action plan.

Participants built a "today" situation—that is, a depiction of the case company's current state. They then created a new model—a vision—that showed what the case company could become. From there, the management team transformed

(continued)

(*continued*)

these individual models of the vision into a shared model of it, and eventually developed the action plan, which they presented to a board consisting of senior and executive vice presidents.

Outcome: The program was a success; 15 out of 16 participants provided the highest available score in the evaluation. It has since moved from the research and development (R&D) division to being a corporate program.

In the words of the program manager in leadership and talent development: "What we saw was that talents who on a day-to-day basis do not have to relate to business strategy or vision for the future, with the LEGO SERIOUS PLAY method were able to work very specifically with dilemmas in the case, and through that experienced how a real executive group must make difficult and complicated choices in establishing and executing a strategy."

A participant described it as "Great fun. The best I've ever tried." Another said, "It was fantastic, especially when it came to something as intangible as the term *vision*. I have never before experienced that there was no frustration due to poor communication in a team. We got the tools to keep an overview and a common thread in the discussion." Still another concurred: "It was great because everyone was active and dedicated to the common result. Furthermore, I am confident that we will be able to remember what we have done for many years. The LEGO SERIOUS PLAY method is the most powerful process I have ever attended."

Case Example # 17: Refocus to Reenter the Workforce

Background: A government program aimed at employees on sick leave due to factors such as stress, anxiety, or depression. This was in most cases caused by factors in their workplace, factors that were beyond their influence or control. The option was to either get the employees to return to their former workplace or find a new field of work or they would ultimately lose their unemployment benefit and as a consequence be on social welfare, which was not a desirable outcome for anyone.

Issue: The employees in the program were highly diverse with regards to their personal background, general education, profession, and motivation. The challenge was to get this group to realize their potential see that despite the failure they felt they had suffered in their workplace/career, they still had lots of potential and the way to regain motivation was to rediscover their potential, refocus and then move on.

LEGO SERIOUS PLAY intervention: The intervention consisted of a series of 1- to 2-hour workshops. The workshops were a mix of self-discovery and new ways of thinking that could help them construct new aspirations for both their personal and work life.

Outcome: The method in this case indeed became a very powerful thinking, communication, and problem-solving technique. For the first time during their sick leave the participants were able to put words to their thoughts and feelings in a form that was safe for all. And the bricks indeed fulfilled their most important role of "helping you build in your mind, when you build in the world." The success rate for these groups in terms of returning to the labor force was remarkably high and many of the participants in the program directly attributed this to the method.

Case Example 18: Defining the Good Life: Muscular Dystrophy Association

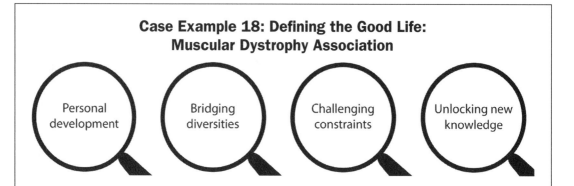

| Personal development | Bridging diversities | Challenging constraints | Unlocking new knowledge |

Background: Muscular dystrophy is a group of diseases impacting the muscles and the central nervous system. It cannot be cured, and slowly disables the patient. An association with members who suffer from muscular dystrophy or are related to someone with the disease was founded in the early 1970s. The association's goal is to help disease sufferers, and those who care for them, to live active lives and take part in society on an equal footing. It also aims to inform about the disease and create a more widespread understanding.

Issue: The disease has an undeniably huge impact on patients, their families, and their life partners. So how does one define the "good life" in such a situation? What does it mean—and how can or how *does* one live it?

LEGO SERIOUS PLAY intervention: Together with the team from the rehabilitation center, a one-day LEGO SERIOUS PLAY workshop was designed for patients and their spouses. Some patients had to bring their caretakers as well, who in some cases even had to play an active part in the building as some patients were largely paralyzed. The group was split in two: patients with patients and spouses with spouses. This was crucial, as spouses were seldom given a voice and rarely had the chance to share their feelings, experiences, and frustrations with people who were enduring a similar experience. A full day ended with each person building his or her version of what the "good life" meant, and what they could do—or stop doing—in order to live it.

Outcome: A very emotional day ended with much clarity for most if not all the participants. Many who had only recently been hit with the disease and were still going through a denial phase found it challenging, yet also liberating. They discovered a new version of what a good life could mean. Participants who had suffered longer had a much-welcomed opportunity to be able to articulate what they felt and to find new meaning in the life they could live.

MISCONCEPTIONS

For many, understanding what LEGO SERIOUS PLAY is and what it does is not intuitive. The LEGO brand and the LEGO bricks lead to associations and misunderstandings. Here, we outline five of the most common ones.

Misconception 1: It Is a Tool for Creativity and Innovation Only

It is a very common assumption—almost a prejudice—that LEGO SERIOUS PLAY is a method primarily related to creativity and innovation development or even teaching people how to *be* innovative. This is simply not the case. While the method is also highly useful for innovation challenges, the users in that field are among the minority. The scope of topics and challenges that the method has been applied to are very broad and continue to expand. Finally, as we have shown throughout this book, it is not a teaching technique.

Misconception 2: It Is a Team-Building Exercise Only

Typically, people who view LEGO SERIOUS PLAY as a team-building exercise confuse it with other techniques using LEGO bricks. They expect the workshop to be a fun break or perhaps a physical activity to kick off a longer session. There are indeed many examples of using LEGO bricks for team building; many of them are good and offer a good laugh or learning point about how the team works together. However, these are not LEGO SERIOUS PLAY; we can compare these with the classic exercise of building a tower or bridge with spaghetti.

Misconception 3: It Is an Icebreaker or a Fun Break (So It Is Not for Serious Business—and Therefore Not for Us)

This is a version of the preceding misconception, but with less focus on the bricks and really no expectations about the outcome. In misconception 2 at least there was the expectation that the team would learn about working together. Here, there are no expectations other than a bit of relaxing fun. As will be clear by now, however, LEGO SERIOUS PLAY is almost the opposite; it is hard fun, and it engages your brain in a playful manner to solve a real problem.

Misconception 4: It Is for Creative People Only (So It Is Not for Me)

As mentioned earlier, the brightly colored LEGO bricks are often a bit of a double-edged sword. Their sheer nature as a toy leads many to think that the method is only for the creative class or people in the creative industries. Few things could be further from the truth. While many people who work in so-called creative industries are used to prototype and use physical objects to model what something may look like, LEGO SERIOUS PLAY is about using the concrete objects to construct new knowledge about the abstract. The process is not about building complicated and artistic models. It is about articulating knowledge and exploring what we know about a given thing. And, as we saw in Chapter 9, the imagination is not something reserved for a few special people. Therefore, no class, group, or educational background is any better suited to the method than others are.

Misconception 5: LEGO Just Wants to Expand Its Market (So There Must Be a Catch, and I Am Not Going to Fall for It)

We have already outlined how the development of LEGO SERIOUS PLAY did not come as the result of some big plan; nor was it developed with a marketing plan up the sleeve. Nevertheless, some still expect this to be the case, so they then look for the catch or wonder about what credibility the LEGO Company has in the consulting market. It doesn't take them long to realize that LEGO SERIOUS PLAY is not just a marketing ploy or extended advertisement for LEGO; it is a serious approach that has helped improve the bottom line for thousands of businesses.

We will now move from looking at how the method has been used in a wide variety of organizations and the misunderstandings that live in the marketplace to how it has been used inside the LEGO Company—and the challenges associated with this particular client.

CHAPTER 12
LEGO® SERIOUS PLAY® at Work in the LEGO Company

In this chapter we look at how, where, and when LEGO SERIOUS PLAY has been used in the LEGO Company as a tool for building a better business. The general assumption we have met has been that the LEGO Company naturally must be a super-user on all levels—and that this method might even have played a key role in the amazing turnaround of the company. It would have been nice if this was the true story. That is, however, not the case. That being said, though, the LEGO Company has been and still is a fairly frequent user of LEGO SERIOUS PLAY and is probably one of the companies in the world that has used and uses it most broadly.

In this chapter we will give multiple examples of how the company has used the methodology across the organization. But before we do that, let us elaborate on four reasons why the LEGO Company has not been a super-user from day one.

1. During the early days of LEGO SERIOUS PLAY, the LEGO Company was going through a very difficult period and had its first CEO who was not a member of the founding family. This CEO had an approach to management and strategy making that was less coherent with LEGO SERIOUS PLAY than the approach Kjeld Kirk Kristiansen stands for. We did in fact use the method with this CEO's executive team a couple of years before he was replaced by the current CEO. The workshop already then gave a clear picture of the challenges the company was facing which later almost cost it its life as an independent family-owned company.

2. LEGO SERIOUS PLAY has never been part of the company's core business and core competencies. It is an idea that was conceived and developed outside the main halls of the LEGO Company's business, and it is still living most of its life outside the LEGO Company. When a leader, manager, or team wants to use it for enterprise or team development, it is an external service they need to pay for like any other external service. That payment even includes paying for the bricks. For many potential users inside the LEGO Company this can be a mental stretch if not an outright disqualifier.

3. The LEGO brick, as previously mentioned, often sends a conflicting signal: it comes across as a toy and indicates children's play. In many ways this signal is even stronger within the LEGO Company. Here the employees know what the

bricks are, and often they may even recognize a particular brick or model as belonging to one or another product line ("Ah, this is from so-and-so box, launched in 20XX and aimed at seven-year-old boys"). For a LEGO employee who has little knowledge of LEGO SERIOUS PLAY, an apparently random collection of bricks used metaphorically looks a lot less impressive than a traditional real-life-looking LEGO model such as the one shown in Figure 12.1, yet is often harder to create. A good portion of the people most challenged with building metaphorical and abstract models (e.g., Figure 12.2) are highly skilled model builders from LEGO.

4. LEGO SERIOUS PLAY has since its origin led a tumultuous life and had several existential crises, as described earlier. It is a history that includes multiple business models, and for long periods of time as a business it has been more or less dormant. This made it more difficult for potential users inside the LEGO Company to know,

FIGURE 12.1   Traditional LEGO Model

FIGURE 12.2   Metaphorical LEGO Model

first, whether LEGO SERIOUS PLAY at a given point in time even was an option to consider and, second, how to get hold of someone who could deliver the service to them. This uncertainty about the business status of the method and the lack of delivery reliability have made many give up on the idea without even trying it.

It started as an uncertain first step, but the use of LEGO SERIOUS PLAY within the LEGO Company has been on a steady increase since 2010. This is a result of more internal awareness, a reliable distribution model that is easily accessible to all, training of a corps of internal facilitators, and the long-term commitment by the LEGO Company to maintaining and supporting the LEGO SERIOUS PLAY concept.

EXAMPLES OF USE WITHIN THE LEGO COMPANY

In Table 12.1 we have gathered a number of examples of how the method has been used inside LEGO, including workshops designed and delivered over a 10-year period, some by internal LEGO employees trained in the method and some by outside facilitators.

TABLE 12.1   LEGO SERIOUS PLAY at Work Inside the LEGO Company

Leadership	Supply Chain and Sourcing	Product and Service Development	Sales and Marketing	Support and Staff
Strategy: Two-day strategy development workshop. **Leadership Values:** One-day personal values exploration workshop. The goal was for leadership team members to share their most important personal values and how these influence their long-term behavior. The outcome was for each member to commit to a set of personal action items as a result of the insight gained in the workshop.	**Vision and Mission:** One-day workshop for departmental management team identifying vision, core identity, and in particular what value they should deliver to the full organization. **Culture:** Half-day workshop on creating the best possible department culture. **Team Development:** Full-day workshop to improve the team's desire and ability to work as *one* team despite organizational, geographical, and cultural barriers.	**Department Mission:** One-day workshop with all 40 employees in a department. Focus was on developing a shared understanding of the department's mission, the key value it should deliver, and what the most important stakeholders were. **Virtual Team Development**: Workshop for a team responsible for direct consumer experiences relationship. Team members were located partly at HQ and partly in the	**Regional Sales Team Strategy:** One-day strategy workshop focusing on developing a mission and vision, and identifying key challenges and personal actions for the team responsible for sales in Latin America. **Culture and Personal Action Plan:** One-day workshop to understand the current way of doing business by building the good, bad, and ugly of today, and with this understanding, to build and commit to an aspiration for the future of	**Vision and Personal Initiatives:** Two-day workshop with the top 40 people in the finance community in LEGO. Delivery was a clear vision for finance and a set of personal initiatives to make this become real. **Team Development:** Full-day team development workshop for a team of lean specialists to get a better understanding of who is on the team, and to develop a culture and behavior that would help the team attain their vision. It was important

TABLE 12.1 (*Continued*)

Leadership	Supply Chain and Sourcing	Product and Service Development	Sales and Marketing	Support and Staff
Empowerment: A workshop to explore the leadership challenge associated with the need to change focus from being operational to being strategic and how to delegate more (i.e., empower people). Through the workshop, leaders from levels 1 and 2 were able to surface both the physical and the mental constraints holding the individual back in regard to changing focus and delegating. **Trust and Respect:** Two-day workshop with	**Health and Safety:** A range of workshops in multiple locations about safety, health, and well-being (SHW). The purpose of the workshops was to involve ground floor personnel in setting concrete goals and initiatives for SHW and thereby build more ownership and thus increase the level of success in achieving the goals. **Operational Efficiency:** Half-day workshop for a cross-functional group with responsibilities	major markets. The goal of the workshop was to increase (almost from zero) the individual team members' knowledge about each other's respon-sibilities, competencies, values, and strengths, in order to improve the team's overall collaboration and collective intelligence. **Strategy and Concept Develop-ment:** Full-day workshop for a group responsible for direct-to-consumer service who needed to align their ideas and	the division's operational culture. The final step in this workshop was for each individual to develop his or her personal action plan for the aspiration. **Identity, Aspiration, and Strategic Priorities:** Two-day workshop involving day 1 the entire department (35 people) and day 2 the leadership team only. Day 1 defined and built commitment to a shared core identity and to an aspiration for the coming years. Day 2 for the leadership	to develop a unique team culture, yet one that was fully aligned with the corporate culture. It finished with the individuals considering what personal change they would have to go through in order to live the new culture. **Induction Program:** Two-day induction programs for new employees. Are held several times each year. LEGO SERIOUS PLAY is an integrated part of the program. The new employees use it to communicate about themselves,

(*Continued*)

TABLE 12.1   *(Continued)*

Leadership	Supply Chain and Sourcing	Product and Service Development	Sales and Marketing	Support and Staff
the primary goals of building more trust and respect, and reducing frustrations by understanding each other's responsibilities and priorities.	for long-term product planning. The group wanted to arrive at a common understanding of the core purpose for the group's work to become more effective with their work. The workshop enabled them to build a shared understanding of the essential mission they were fulfilling with their work.	efforts and commit to a shared strategy for both content and process. The workshop included defining a six-month aspiration, testing what-if scenarios, building team spirit, and committing to taking responsibility for concrete actions.	team took the day 1 results further and explored the wider strategic consequences in order to ultimately determine priorities for years 1 and 2.	their passions, values, and competencies, and to express their perceptions of the LEGO brand values. **Exploring the Future**: Half-day workshop for 250 employees from corporate IT and the IT service center. The purpose was to build 10 scenarios and imagine how the future of the wider world (the consumer world, and the LEGO world) will impact IT and how IT can prepare to deal with these changes.

TABLE 12.1   (*Continued*)

Leadership	Supply Chain and Sourcing	Product and Service Development	Sales and Marketing	Support and Staff
				Department Strategy: Two-day workshop developing the IT department's strategy and vision.

The table shows how LEGO SERIOUS PLAY can be used broadly within a company on many different levels and for groups of varying size.

LEGO SERIOUS PLAY was developed to help LEGO build a better business. In this chapter we have reflected on why using it in this organization posed particular problems, yet still matured into using the method broadly. In the previous chapter we focused on how it has been used for business purposes in a variety of organizations from all over the world. The next chapter will look at how the method has been used for something more or different than building better businesses or better organizations.

CHAPTER 13

LEGO® SERIOUS PLAY® at Work outside Business

Most of what we've covered so far throughout this book has to do with using LEGO SERIOUS PLAY for business. And while this purpose is what has driven much of the method's development, that doesn't mean that the use of LEGO SERIOUS PLAY has been or is limited to this field. There is nothing in the method itself that excludes people from other fields and from applying it contexts other than business. Indeed, it is relevant to and applicable in *any* situation where leaders want people to lean forward, unlock new knowledge, and break habitual thinking.

Some other applications include:

- Education for elementary, middle, and high school
- Undergraduate and graduate education, including business schools
- As a qualitative interview technique in research
- Focus groups and observational research
- Group therapy for families
- Family life and family team building
- Life coaching for individuals and groups
- Children's summer camps
- Retirement planning for seniors
- As an interview technique for journalists

The applications all share the same motivation for using LEGO SERIOUS PLAY: they are drawn to the method's unique ability to combine a number of key features into a practical approach:

- Everyone can master the process of building with LEGO bricks.
- It puts everyone on a level playing field—both the quiet and the dominating, the language proficient and the less proficient.

- It gets everyone involved continuously. It is not possible for anyone not to be part of what is going on (i.e., to withdraw into their own world).
- Because participants always have to build their answers before anyone starts talking, it encourages the revelation of people's authentic insights, and hinders the influence of individual opinions and perspectives about the matters being explored.
- It prioritizes facilitating self-learning over teaching and instruction.

The greatest number of experiences with LEGO SERIOUS PLAY outside the business world have taken place within the educational and research fields. Therefore, we will go more in-depth with these two categories.

LEGO SERIOUS PLAY IN EDUCATION

Given Robert's background in and connections to education, it seemed natural to wonder whether the method would work with children. In the spirit of LEGO SERIOUS PLAY, there was only one thing to do: try it out.

Once we did, the conclusion rapidly became clear: if the purpose is to explore and learn rather than teach, then it works very well with children as young as six and seven years old, even from a variety of different cultures. Apart from having to explain a little more about metaphors and elaborate on how they are using the LEGO bricks to tell stories instead of building a model of something, the process works the same as for adults. Older students who had stopped playing with LEGO several years ago found it motivating as well. As one 14-year-old stated, "I thought I had outgrown playing with LEGO. . . but I like how you can build things that aren't concrete, such as what is a good morning in my family or what friendship is." A teacher who has used LEGO SERIOUS PLAY for multiple projects in middle school ranging from nutrition and health to literature and book reports refers to Gregory Bateson's writings as one of her inspirations for using the method by quoting the following: "Not until I have said what I am thinking can I think about what I am saying."

A leading school in applying LEGO SERIOUS PLAY to education is A.B. Combs Leadership Magnet Elementary School in Raleigh, North Carolina. Here are three examples from their curriculum:

1. After completing a class read aloud, students use the process to build their favorite scene from the book, most memorable event, or a model that represents the problem/solution of the story.
2. When talking about emotional bank accounts (EBAs), students build a model that represents a way someone can make a deposit in the EBA, and then after a discussion students build a model representing a withdrawal from their EBA.
3. When teaching point of view/perspective, students build a model to represent the two sides and compare and contrast.

LEGO SERIOUS PLAY has also found success at the college and university level, including undergraduate, graduate, and executive business education. We can best describe this segment's users as those also interested in *action learning*, which can be described as "an educational process in which the student performs an activity and then studies it in order to improve their performance. In an action learning environment that typically occurs in small groups or sets, students pick up experience by repeatedly performing actions and then obtain feedback by analyzing their actions (www .businessdictionary.com).

Like John Dewey's learning by doing approach, the action learning theory makes a great deal of sense. And while it makes sense to implement this tactic in a variety of situations, things get a little more complicated when it comes to figuring out exactly *how* to do so. For those in education, LEGO SERIOUS PLAY is a highly relevant answer to the challenge of implementing real action learning. Users of the method in business schools, MBA programs, and executive education often have a dual purpose: they want to reap the benefits for current interaction, but also want to expose their students to a method that has relevance for the companies in which they work or will be working once they finish their education.

The list of applications for this group includes the following topics:

- Reflecting upon and discussing different aspects of teaching, learning, and curriculum
- Kicking off, evaluating, and providing feedback for student projects
- Defining content and expectations for educational programs
- Team building among students
- Identifying students' needs and expectations
- Forming focus groups to capture the student experience
- Developing students' skills at learning how to learn
- Creating learning communities
- Generating ideas for educational projects

LEGO SERIOUS PLAY IN RESEARCH

The use of LEGO SERIOUS PLAY in the field of research is often closely related to its use in college- and university-level education. Undergraduate and postgraduate students might employ the method for observational research and data collection, or professors might use it as a component of research into the usability of alternative ways of teaching and/or learning. There is also a growing interest in initiating research into the actual end-user impact of LEGO SERIOUS PLAY and developing a deeper understanding of the science component. This might be in the domain related to learning and development (e.g., neuroscience) or in how the method impacts the development of business challenges, such as forming innovation teams or creating new visions (e.g., Louise Møller Nielsen, *Personal and Shared Experiential Concepts*, and Volker Grienitz, André-Marcel Schmidt, Per Kristiansen, and Helmut Schulte, "Vision Statement Development with LEGO SERIOUS PLAY"[1]).

A very small snapshot of higher education institutions that use or have used LEGO SERIOUS PLAY includes:

- University of Twente, The Netherlands
- University of Siegen, Germany
- Chemnitz University of Technology, Germany
- IMD, Lausanne, Switzerland
- Universita Svizzera Italiana, Switzerland
- Globis School of Management, Tokyo, Japan
- New York University Stern School of Business, United States
- Harvard Business School, Executive Education, Boston, United States
- Simmons School of Management, Boston, United States
- Wharton School, Philadelphia, United States
- Imperial College, London, United Kingdom
- London Business School, United Kingdom
- London College of Fashion, United Kingdom
- University of Aalborg, Denmark
- Copenhagen Business School, Denmark
- Escuela Universitaria Real Madrid, Spain
- Tecnologico de Monterey, Mexico
- Universidad Tecnologica del Poniente, Mexico
- Waikato Management School, New Zealand
- University of Queensland, Australia

An example is from Escuela Universitaria Real Madrid, which has an MBA progam in sports management. In that program LEGO SERIOUS PLAY is used for two purposes in the second part of the program.

First, it is used to prepare the students for working together in project teams. Through the process they learn how to benefit from each other's strengths and how to increase the team's collective intelligence.

Second, the students use the method to define their expectations for their grand study tour, which is meeting in New York with the major U.S. professional sports leagues such as the National Football League (NFL), National Hockey League (NHL), Major League Baseball (MLB), and National Basketball Association (NBA). The outcome of the LEGO SERIOUS PLAY exercise is used by the professors as part of their planning.

There are two other interesting but rather different publications that delve further into the topic of using it or similar methods in education and research: David Gauntlett's book *Creative Explorations* (Routledge, 2007) and *Achieving Participatory Development Communication through 3D Model Building* by Lauren Leigh Hinthorne (Centre for Communication and Social Change, University of Queensland, 2012).

Gauntlett's work explores the ways in which researchers can embrace people's everyday creativity in order to understand social experience. Seeking an alternative to traditional interviews and focus groups, he outlines studies that have required people to make visual things such as video, collage, and drawing and then interpret them. This research led to an innovative project wherein Gauntlett asked people to use LEGO SERIOUS PLAY to build metaphorical models of their identities. His creative, reflective method provides insights into how individuals present themselves, understand their own life stories, and connect with the social world. In his conclusion of the study, Gauntlett writes: "I was surprised [at] the degree of clarity with which a wide range of people could picture their own 'identity,' on their own terms, and share this story with others. It has also been heartening, if not so surprising, to find that people are philosophers on the state of their own lives before the social theorists come along."

Lauren Leigh Hinthorne took the method into new and rather uncharted waters when she used it as a tool for participatory development communication. In her own words, she conducted "a provisional situation analysis with key stakeholder groups of the ACIAR [Australian Centre for International Agricultural Research]-funded enhancing smallholder cattle production in East Timor initiative." In short, she brought the method to an area and a population that had never seen LEGO bricks before. Her aim was to solicit feedback and input from the cattle holders to help them get the right kind of development aid.

Participants were village leaders and farmers/cattle holders. The exercises included asking the participants to build models expressing their perceptions of the livestock management practices currently in use. They were then asked to build their vision of what improved livestock management might look like and what resources they would need to achieve this hoped-for state.

Among her observations, Lauren Leigh Hinthorne notes the high quality of participant engagement and the space the method created for participants to work through a problem. She emphasizes how the approach helped the participants deconstruct what would otherwise have been a highly complex situation.

After having looked at how the use of LEGO SERIOUS PLAY has evolved with success into areas for which it was not originally intended, let's continue with a chapter offering some reflections about what to be conscious about when putting the process to work.

CHAPTER 14
Contemplating LEGO® SERIOUS PLAY® at Work

Three things stand out very clearly to us after more than a decade of working with LEGO SERIOUS PLAY.

1. It works across a very broad range of industries and areas.
2. It works for every person in any culture.
3. All workshops are customized.

Let's examine these three observations.

IT WORKS ACROSS A VERY BROAD RANGE OF INDUSTRIES AND AREAS

We hope that the cases we have shared make it clear that the method works across many areas. Though created for strategy development in a family-owned toy company in Denmark, it has evolved into a thinking and communication method whose applicability is limited only by the nature of the problem and the beliefs of the organization seeking to solve that problem. As we have shown, it has worked well in organizations large and small, private and public, for-profit and nonprofit, as well as in education and in research.

We usually encounter limits in the nature of the challenges the organization wants to work on, and in how the organization works. LEGO SERIOUS PLAY is most effective when the challenge is a complex one with no obvious solution.

It takes a courageous manager to introduce LEGO SERIOUS PLAY. He or she has to be brave enough not only to bring in the LEGO bricks, but also to open up a very candid dialogue that will allow everyone present to speak their mind. There is an element of relinquishing control for a period of time. It takes courage to enter into a process where one allows oneself and one's convictions to be challenged. However, it is not enough that the manager in question is courageous; he or she also should be part of an organization—that is, a culture—that believes in the potential of its people, and allows its employees to act and think strategically. And in the words of Kjeld Kirk Kristiansen, owner of LEGO, in a 2002 interview, "Unfortunately, not all organizations are ready for LEGO SERIOUS PLAY."

IT WORKS FOR EVERY PERSON IN ANY CULTURE

The method can work for everyone. It does not have any specific prerequisites for certain individuals; workshop participants do not have to have played with LEGO bricks before, or need to consider themselves creative. They don't need to come from a particular national culture or religious belief system. And though it may seem surprising, even physical abilities (or lack thereof) don't seem to play much of a role. We've done workshops with participants who have paralyzed limbs, who were visually impaired, or who suffered from muscular dystrophy. As mentioned earlier, the only thing that limits the method is the context in which it is used—the nature of the challenge and the organization where the workshop takes place.

ALL WORKSHOPS ARE CUSTOMIZED

The fact that LEGO SERIOUS PLAY is a method and a language to solve all kind of problems became evident during the first years of using it. Initially, we saw it is as *one* workshop created to develop a dynamic strategy. This process took two days and the boxes used carried the name of this process: LEGO SERIOUS PLAY Real Time Strategy for the Enterprise. We even developed a beautiful booklet (*The Imaginopedia for Real Time Strategy for the Enterprise*) to support the process. But while this was—and still is—a good workshop, it became clear that this concept of one size fits all in fact rarely fit anyone; very few were looking for the exact result it had to offer. Consequently, the need for more diverse applications became evident.

The initial response from the Executive Discovery team was to develop two more standard workshops for team development and personal development. LEGO SERIOUS PLAY became defined by *three* workshops with supporting materials. Yet every time we had designed the flow of a new workshop, new adaptations emerged, and it became clear to us that the LEGO SERIOUS PLAY method is not one, two, or three standard workshops. Rather, it is a method that not only *can* but also *must be* customized.

We still train facilitators in the standard road maps for the strategy and the team workshops, but we do so to give them the tools and techniques to work most effectively within the parameters of these particular workshops. Our main focus now is for the facilitators to learn how to use the Core Process and seven Application Techniques to design unique workshops.

PITFALLS

Is the conclusion then that LEGO SERIOUS PLAY is a panacea that works for everyone, all the time and everywhere? It is tempting to say yes—especially for us—but the proper answer is no. We've already shared some of the limits, and discussed facilitator traps in detail in Chapter 4. In addition to these, we identify here five pitfalls for both the organization and the facilitator to look out for. Falling into any one of these could lead to a situation in which not everyone is leaning in, habitual patterns of thinking are not being broken, and new insights are not emerging.

1. *Gaming the play*. Like when children play, one person can try to game the play and consequently undermine it. This becomes obvious very quickly in LEGO SERIOUS PLAY; either the person is clearly obstructing by not following the method (e.g., ignoring questions or deliberately misunderstanding them) or he or she is not "playing with open cards." The latter often comes in the form of not being fully honest or even being outright *dis*honest. The other participants or the facilitator will almost always pick up on this, and the facilitator will then need to handle the situation. It's often quite simple to hear or see; some signs include a participant leaning back a bit more, talking in the third person, and/or deviating from the model. When gaming is not stopped, the method is undermined and in the end falls apart.
2. *"I have the answer."* Sometimes it's the case that someone—usually a manager or sponsor—is convinced that he or she has the answer, and wants to use this fun and creative method to convey his or her opinion rather than seeking others' input. If a key person brings this kind of attitude into the workshop, then it doesn't

have much chance of surviving. The person will feel that the other participants are challenging his or her position and point of view. In turn, the other participants will feel manipulated and will likely wonder why their opinion is being asked for when the top dog is not listening. In short, we always tell people that if you know the answer, then don't waste time building. LEGO SERIOUS PLAY is not about what you already consciously know; it is about unlocking new knowledge.

3. *Do we want to open this up?* If senior managers do not want to open up the discussion and the solution, then it will never work. The method is based on an open dialogue where there are no sacred cows that cannot be mentioned and turned into LEGO models.

4. *Do we want to be asked or told?* The method is based on questions that bring answers to the surface. The questions come from an *outsider* (the facilitator), and the answers come from the *insiders* (the participants). If the organization is expressly seeking or expecting expert advice, outside-in inspiration, or teaching, then the approach won't work for its situation, since the organization won't get what it is looking for.

5. *Observers.* One may consider having observers for a number of reasons, and they may be appropriate in a number of interventions; however, LEGO SERIOUS PLAY is not one of them. When participants are being observed, they will typically either consciously or unconsciously alter behavior—perhaps by not sharing everything they know. Similar to what we saw in pitfall 1, this also resembles children's play—which is easy to see upon watching actual children play. Observe how long it takes for children to change their behavior once they become aware of the fact that you're watching them. The play stops, they become more hesitant, or they may even ask for your help where they otherwise would not. This pitfall is also reminiscent of Heisenberg's uncertainty principle: you cannot observe a system without it changing behavior.

Till now we've shared with you the territory of LEGO SERIOUS PLAY, looked at the theories that inform how the method works, and seen where and how it has been applied. In the next and final chapter we will close the book with exploring which boundaries LEGO SERIOUS PLAY may push, and how it might push them.

CHAPTER 15
Pushing the Boundaries with LEGO® SERIOUS PLAY®

In the previous 14 chapters we have outlined the territory that defines the LEGO SERIOUS PLAY method, the theories supporting and informing it, and finally where and how it is being applied. Now we want to conclude with reflecting on how it can help push boundaries. What these boundaries are we will explore later in this chapter. First, a little bit of context.

Since the inception of LEGO SERIOUS PLAY at the end of the previous century, the world has undergone many changes. Currently, it is facing numerous challenges with an economy that has gone from exuberantly high to depressingly low and is now in a state of cautious optimism. During its life span over the past 15 years, the method has been much more widely used in the period since the world economy hit its low in 2008 than the one before when economic growth seemed to be a given. Only a part of this difference in the usage of LEGO SERIOUS PLAY can be attributed to the new community distribution model. Since it is our belief that the new business model only partly explains the traction that it is gaining, we will not, in the following pages, be reflecting upon how to push the boundaries of the LEGO SERIOUS PLAY method itself, but upon which boundaries we see the method being able to push in future development of businesses and society in general.

This may be surprising since we live in a period that is in love with anything that is new (some would claim that our society collectively suffers from "neomania"), and, therefore, one could have expected us to hypothesize about how new technology can push LEGO SERIOUS PLAY into being something else.

However, LEGO SERIOUS PLAY has been around for more than a decade largely without changing, and if we follow the argument of proportionality of life expectancy for something nonperishable, then the method has at least another decade of existence ahead of it. In the words of provocateur-academic and scholar Nassim Nicholas Taleb: "For the perishable, every additional day in its life translates into a *shorter* additional life expectancy. For the nonperishable, every additional day may imply a *longer* life expectancy."[1]

In our opinion, there are three main reasons why LEGO SERIOUS PLAY may have a vibrant future ahead of it: (1) the need for getting people to lean forward, unlock knowledge, and break habitual habits will not be diminishing (on the contrary);

(2) LEGO SERIOUS PLAY can tap into the genetically programmed and natural way for humans to think, communicate, problem solve, and express thoughts and ideas through a process that involves the use of hands; and finally (3) LEGO SERIOUS PLAY is able to push some of the important boundaries that businesses and society in general will need to push in the coming decade:

- Pushing past the challenges of dynamic complexity
- Pushing past death by data
- Pushing past "what got you here won't get me there"
- Pushing past high-tech myopia
- Pushing past hero leadership
- Pushing past relying on individual genius
- Pushing past the carrot-and-stick approach

Next we will look more closely at the boundaries that we believe LEGO SERIOUS PLAY will be pushing in the decade to come.

PUSHING PAST THE CHALLENGES OF DYNAMIC COMPLEXITY

Scholars like C. Otto Scharmer are arguing that we are going into a period defined by dynamic complexity. In Scharmer's words, a distance between cause and effect characterizes dynamic complexity and as a consequence it is no longer enough to learn from the past; we need to start learning from the future as it emerges.[2] This is close to the line of argument we presented in Chapter 1 when we spoke about complex adaptive systems thinking; here scholars typically would say that in order to maneuver, one needs to probe the system, observe, learn, and then act.

Returning to Scharmer, he argues that if we want to learn from the emerging future we need to shift our conversation (and awareness) from (1) downloading—talking nice, (2) debating—talking tough, and (3) dialogue—reflective inquiry, to finally (4) collective presence, in which the group cocreates something new.[3]

It is our experience that a well-conducted LEGO SERIOUS PLAY workshop can do exactly this. During the opening skills-building challenges, participants already move beyond the empty and polite phrases; then in the early building rounds (Application Technique 1) they move from exchanging divergent views and defending these toward seeing themselves as part of an adaptive system and finally in the later stages of the workshop they start cocreating a new and larger whole.

PUSHING PAST DEATH BY DATA

It is no secret that we never before had access to as much data as we have now. The opportunities for collecting data through, for example, web traffic and use of smartphones (where and when) combined with their processing power present businesses with what seem to be endless opportunities, opportunities that will probably be dwarfed by what will be available in a few years. Consequently, numerous approaches in the manner of analytics have emerged, all celebrating this. But is big data the business equivalent of the philosopher's stone? We are not certain; we have mentioned previously (in Chapter 1 of this book) that in their "invisible gorilla" test Chabris and Simons showed how we as observers can miss what should be obvious if we are focused on collecting one particular kind of data,[4] and in *Antifragile* Nassim Nicholas Taleb makes a similar point:

> We have never had more data than we have now, yet have less predictability than ever. More data—such as paying attention to the eye colors of the people around [you] when crossing the street—can make you miss the big truck.

We deeply believe that a method like LEGO SERIOUS PLAY can help everyone push past the data; it can help construct new knowledge and surprising insights. Building the intangible into physical models, and articulating and visualizing data can help us see what we may otherwise be missing, and find the surprising patterns.

PUSHING PAST "WHAT GOT YOU HERE WON'T GET ME THERE"

In many parts of the world the economy is stagnating. As the Danish proverb goes, "There is an upper limit to everything" (or, as we say: "The trees don't grow into heaven"), and it seems that in many places a limit has been reached, yet simultaneously in other parts of the world many countries are looking for growth. These countries are often trying to find their own path leading to growth. There is an increasing feeling that the approach to management and capitalism that historically fueled the growth in Europe and North America may not be what will help companies in developing economies grow, and even in these (let's call them old-world economies), we experience a growing interest in creating something new, a different way of managing. The LEGO SERIOUS PLAY approach proposes that creating leaning-in meetings that lead to unlocking new knowledge and breaking habitual patterns could be exactly such a way of managing. Growth is no longer a given, and as Albert Einstein allegedly said:

Insanity: doing the same thing over and over again and expecting different results.

We cannot solve our problems with the same thinking we used when we created them.

PUSHING PAST HIGH-TECH MYOPIA

This is not to say that new technology does not hold great promise, as undoubtedly it does. But, just as collecting more data and processing it, high tech is not necessarily the answer to what can create better and more meaningful lives and better businesses. New technology is making things easier in many aspects of life, and increasingly it is making a number of activities time and space independent, which is a great gift for most of us. However, while technology may be seen as the great equalizer, it may also have two other effects: (1) it becomes hard to be distinct and harder to avoid commoditizing, and (2) if we do not meet very often in person, we expect even more from when we actually do meet.

We believe that LEGO SERIOUS PLAY can be part of pushing past these two effects. Unlocking new knowledge and breaking habitual patterns of thinking can help teams unleash their imagination and find their own uniqueness. This is also where teams push beyond the data. And truly creating leaning-in meetings where the 20/80 dynamic is broken creates real conversation and real cocreation. We have previously mentioned how we see a dual movement: two trends happening simultaneously, one going toward more high tech and one going toward more high touch. It is this latter trend that we believe will create a sweet spot for this method.

PUSHING PAST HERO LEADERSHIP

One of the major benefits of LEGO SERIOUS PLAY, mentioned over and over, is the ability to break the 20/80 meeting curse and create a process that is fair and where everyone is equal.

So why is the method able to break this curse by bringing equality to the table? Dutch evolutionary biologist Mark van Vugt's research about the evolutionary science of leadership may provide insight. In his 2011 book *Naturally Selected: The Evolutionary Science of Leadership*, van Vugt makes a convincing case that current management theories and practices have evolved more rapidly than our brains.[5] Deep in our brains lives a primal, natural sense of right and wrong, what makes sense, and what seems irrational. Stone Age men and women bonded together in tribes. Many aspects of how and why members of a tribe worked together and thrived still make sense in today's fast-paced, complex, and chaotic world. Leadership for Stone Age people was trust based. Tribes rarely exceeded between 150 and 200 members, so people knew each other really well, and their relationships were close and informal. Relationships among and between early humans were more equal because in primitive societies it was difficult to accumulate resources and power.

According to van Vugt, the principle of equality is still an important part of our instincts. Large organizations can kill motivation. In some large hierarchical organizations, top leaders can earn as much as 380 times the pay of an entry-level employee. This wide range in compensation feels unnatural and alienating, deepening the frustration among average employees. In our ancestors' time, leaders were usually democratically selected. Today's average employee has little or no influence over leader selection. And instead of leadership being situational, or project specific, many leaders hold universal power.

When employees are accustomed to working in a hierarchical system, it is challenging to relax into a more natural leadership model where people know and trust each other, and share leadership responsibilities according to the tasks at hand. A key insight from our work with large organizations is that the equal and democratic nature of the LEGO SERIOUS PLAY process can reconnect all employees with their own deep knowledge and create a better foundation for natural leadership to emerge and flourish.

PUSHING PAST RELYING ON INDIVIDUAL GENIUS

As expertise becomes more specialized, almost all problems and projects require the insights of at least several individuals. Often the individuals assembled are from varying professional domains, a range of generations, and even different countries. The ability to work effectively with others will therefore become fundamental to the success of projects, programs, and enterprises in every sector of the global economy.

Keith Sawyer's *Group Genius* (2007) has given us powerful case-study examples of the merits of harnessing collective intelligence.[6] And many of us have experienced the benefit of collective intelligence. A team of researchers from the Massachusetts Institute of Technology (MIT), Union College, and Carnegie Mellon University used a system of statistical analysis, similar to an IQ test, to demonstrate that collective intelligence (the c-factor) exists, and the c-factor can be measured. In two studies, 699 individuals, working in groups ranging in size from two to five, were surveyed and observed performing a wide range of tasks, including architectural design, brainstorming, group matrix reasoning, group moral reasoning, planning a short trip, and group typing.

Surprisingly, neither average group member intelligence nor maximum member intelligence was a significant predictor of group success. However, there were definite correlations between the c-factor and the group's social sensitivity and turn-taking abilities.

These are also the key characteristics for the LEGO SERIOUS PLAY Core Process, and we believe the future is bright for those organizations that understand how to leverage their c-factor instead of relying on expert knowledge that can easily become outdated.

PUSHING PAST THE CARROT-AND-STICK APPROACH

Most people believe that the best way to motivate is with rewards like money—the carrot-and-stick approach. That's a mistake, according to Daniel H. Pink, the author of *Drive: The Surprising Truth about Motivating Others*.[7] He asserts that the secret to high performance and satisfaction—at work, at school, and at home—is the deeply human need to direct our own lives, to learn and create new things, and to do better by ourselves and our world.

Behavioral economist Daniel Ariely also speaks on what makes us feel good about work. The short answer is that doing meaningful work makes us feel good.[8] But what exactly is meaningful work, and why do we care? His research supports the view that we don't work just for the money. We're partly motivated by money; but when all else is equal, we'd rather be doing meaningful work.

There is plenty of other research that supports Daniel Pink's and Daniel Ariely's claims. As for why that is the case, a key reason is that we have a deep human desire to make and create things. It is the same desire that makes the generated content on the web continue to swell. More than ever before, we are being empowered with the tools, time, and inclination to create things.

LEGO SERIOUS PLAY is more meaningful to people than many other ways of thinking, communicating, and problem solving. It always takes as its starting point the individual person and what is meaningful for this person. It is the builder's meaning in the model and it's the builder's meaning in the story. In this process the builder directs his or her "life" in the workshop, creates his or her own new learning, and ultimately sees the fruits of his or her labor.

As LEGO SERIOUS PLAY continues to take off, we are convinced that it will be pushing past more boundaries and push for more changes. We would like you to end reading this book by going back to the image of a 747 on its way down the runway, and simultaneously think about how it goes against common sense that such a monumental weight can lift itself off the ground. Yet you know it will and it will do so with grace. When we began our journey with LEGO SERIOUS PLAY we had the same thoughts.

Then we didn't know why or how it could fly. However, we know today and we hope we have been able to share this magic with you.

Notes

Chapter 1   The Need for Building Better Businesses

1. Christopher Chabris and Daniel Simons, *The Invisible Gorilla* (New York: Crown, 2010); www.theinvisiblegorilla.com.

Chapter 2   The LEGO® Brick

1. David Robertson, *Brick by Brick* (New York: Crown Business, 2013).
2. Ibid.
3. Donald Schön, *Beyond the Stable State* (New York: Random House, 1971).
4. Ibid.
5. Gareth Morgan, *Images of Organization* (Newbury Park, CA: Sage, 1986).

Chapter 3   Defining Serious Play

1. Johan Huizinga, *Homo Ludens* (London: Routledge & Kegan Paul, 1949; Boston: Beacon Press, 1955).
2. Johan Huizinga, 1938 and 1955, in David Gauntlett and Bo Stjerne Thomsen, *Cultures of Creativity* (Billund: LEGO Foundation, 2013).
3. Stuart Brown, *Play* (New York: Avery, 2009).
4. Roger Caillois, *Man, Play, and Games* (New York: Free Press, 1958; Urbana: University of Illinois Press, 2001).

Chapter 6   Building Knowledge—Giving Your Mind a Hand

1. Seymour Papert, *The Children's Machine* (New York, NY: Basic Books, 1993).
2. Seymour Papert and Idit Harel, *Constructionism* (Norwood, NJ: Ablex Publishing Corporation, 1991).
3. Ibid.
4. Frank Wilson, *The Hand: How Its Use Shapes the Brain, Language and Human Culture* (New York: Pantheon, 1998).
5. Hans Furth, *Piaget and Knowledge: Theoretical Foundations* (Prentice-Hall, 1969).
6. Ferris Jabr, "The Science of Paper versus Screens," *Scientific American*, April 13, 2013.

Chapter 7   Neuroscience—Understanding the Builder's Mind

1. Lila Davachi, Tobias Kiefer, David Rock, and Lisa Rock, "Learning That Lasts through Ages," *NeuroLeadership Journal* 3, 2010.
2. Ibid.
3. Eric Jensen 2005 in *NeuroLeadership Journal* 3, 2010.
4. Theodore W. Wills et al. 2000 in Mark Jung-Beeman, Axurii Collier, and John Kounios, "How Insight Happens: Learning from the Brain," *NeuroLeadership Journal* 1, 2008.

Chapter 8   Flow—The Joy of Effective Learning

1. Hans Henrik Knoop, *Play, Learning and Creativity: Why Happy Children Are Better Learners* (Copenhagen: Aschehoug, 2002).

Chapter 9   Imagination—Seeing What Is Not

1. http://online.wsj.com/news/articles/SB120994652485566323 / *Wall Street Journal*, 2008.
2. Gary Hamel, *Competing for the Future* (Cambridge, MA: Harvard Business Press, 1995).
3. Joe Sharkey, "Reinventing the Suitcase by Adding the Wheel," *New York Times*, October 4, 2010, www.nytimes.com/2010/10/05/business/05road.html?_r=0.
4. Michael Hammer, *The Reengineering Revolution* (New York: HarperCollins, 1995), 4.

Chapter 10   Play Is about Process

1. Johan Huizinga, *Homo Ludens* (London: Routledge & Kegan Paul, 1949; Boston: Beacon Press, 1955).
2. Stuart Brown, *Play* (New York: Avery, 2009).
3. Ibid.
4. Ibid.
5. David Gauntlett and Bo Stjerne Thomsen, *Cultures of Creativity* (Billund: LEGO Foundation, 2013).
6. Brian Sutton-Smith, *The Ambiguity of Play* (Cambridge, MA: Harvard University Press, 2001).
7. Gauntlett and Thomsen, *Cultures of Creativity* (Billund: LEGO Foundation, 2013).
8. Nassim Nicholas Taleb, *Antifragile* (New York: Random House, 2012).

Chapter 13   LEGO® SERIOUS PLAY® at Work outside Business

1. Louise Møller Nielsen, *Personal and Shared Experiential Concepts* (Aalborg University, Denmark, 2009), and Volker Grienitz, André-Marcel Schmidt, Per Kristiansen, and Helmut Schulte, "Vision Statement Development with LEGO SERIOUS PLAY," proceedings of the 2013 Industrial and Systems Engineering Research Conference, San Juan, Puerto Rico.

Chapter 15   Pushing the Boundaries with LEGO® SERIOUS PLAY®

1. Nassim Nicholas Taleb, *Antifragile* (New York: Random House, 2012).
2. C. Otto Scharmer, *Theory U: Leading from the Emerging Future as It Emerges: The Social Technology of Presencing* (San Francisco: Berrett-Koehler, 2007).
3. Ibid.
4. Christopher Chabris and Daniel Simons, *The Invisible Gorilla* (New York: Crown, 2010); www.theinvisiblegorilla.com.
5. Mark van Vugt, *Naturally Selected: The Evolutionary Science of Leadership* (New York: HarperCollins, 2011).
6. Keith Sawyer, *Group Genius* (New York: Basic Books, 2007).
7. Daniel H. Pink, *Drive: The Surprising Truth about What Motivates Us* (New York: Riverhead Books, 2009).
8. Daniel Ariely, http://ed.ted.com/lessons/what-makes-us-feel-good-about-our-work-dan-ariely.

About the Authors

Robert Rasmussen and Per Kristiansen have worked with LEGO® SERIOUS PLAY® since its very beginning. They are the master trainers in the LEGO SERIOUS PLAY method, and both deliver facilitator training programs as well as end-user workshops through their companies Rasmussen Consulting and Trivium in Europe, the United States, Latin America, and Asia. They have written several articles about LEGO SERIOUS PLAY, but *Building a Better Business Using the LEGO® SERIOUS PLAY® Method* is their first book.

Robert Rasmussen worked for the LEGO Group from 1988 to 2001 as head of research and development (R&D) for LEGO Education, and was, among other roles, head of the educational development team for LEGO Mindstorms, the LEGO Company's best-selling product ever. From 2001 to 2004 Robert managed Executive Discovery Ltd., which developed and launched the LEGO SERIOUS PLAY program. He is the main architect of the LEGO SERIOUS PLAY method. After several years and more than 20 iterations, he and his team developed the concept into the reproducible and robust methodology it is today.

Robert is a native of Denmark. He has a master's degree in education and has studied psychology and sociology. He has spent his career applying experiences and theories about learning, teaching, creativity, and play to education and organizational development. Over a 15-year period he worked extensively with designers and researchers at Tufts University and the MIT Media Lab in Boston, Massachusetts, to develop and apply hands-on learning tools. Robert lives with his wife Jette in Assens, Denmark.

Per Kristiansen joined Trivium in 2006, prior to which for a brief spell he had been part of the leadership team at Danfoss Universe, a unique science park that also offers innovation processes to organizations. The LEGO SERIOUS PLAY method was part of the park's activities.

Per has spent a number of years working in the LEGO Group, first as change agent in the preschool area, where he was the right hand of the global brand director. He then joined the LEGO SERIOUS PLAY activities, initially at Executive Discovery, the start-up that developed and managed the method, and later in the LEGO Company. Initially Per's role was two-pronged: (1) master trainer together with Robert and (2) responsible for LEGO SERIOUS PLAY in Europe and the Middle East. When Executive Discovery had been closed down and LEGO SERIOUS PLAY became part of LEGO, Per took on the role of global manager of LEGO SERIOUS PLAY.

Per has a master's degree in intercultural business, and has spent his career helping companies accelerate change and innovation, and in developing robust strategies. He has been based and worked in Italy, Scandinavia, and the United Kingdom. He now lives in Copenhagen with his partner Christina and their two sons.

Index